MW01064710

EUROPEAN SECURITY AND
THE FORMER SOVIET UNION

The Royal Institute of International Affairs is an independent body which promotes the rigorous study of international questions and does not express opinions of its own. The opinions expressed in this publication are the responsibility of the author.

EUROPEAN SECURITY AND THE FORMER SOVIET UNION

Dangers, Opportunities and Gambles

Trevor Taylor

THE ROYAL INSTITUTE OF
INTERNATIONAL AFFAIRS
International Security Programme

© Royal Institute of International Affairs, 1994

Published in Great Britain in 1994 by the Royal Institute of International Affairs, Chatham House, 10 St James's Square, London SW1Y 4LE.

Distributed worldwide by The Brookings Institution, 1775 Massachusetts Avenue, Northwest, Washington, DC 20036-2188, USA.

All rights reserved. No part of this publication may be reproduced, stored in a retrieval system, or transmitted by any other means without the prior written permission of the copyright holder. Please direct all inquiries to the publishers.

British Library Cataloguing in Publication Data
A CIP catalogue record for this book is available from the British Library.

ISBN 0 905031 75 X

Text set in Bembo.
Printed and bound in Great Britain by Redwood Books.

CONTENTS

Tables

ABBREVIATIONS

ABM	Anti-Ballistic Missile (Treaty)
ACV	Armoured Combat Vehicle
AWACS	Airborne Warning and Control System
BMD	Ballistic Missile Defence
CDU	Christian Democratic Union
CFE	Conventional Forces in Europe (Treaty)
CIS	Commonwealth of Independent States
Cocom	Coordinating Committee for Export Controls
CSCE	Conference for Security and Cooperation in Europe
CWC	Chemical Weapons Convention
EBRD	European Bank for Reconstruction and Development
EU	European Union
FSU	Former Soviet Union
G5/G7	Group of 5/Group of 7
GPS	Global Protection System
GUSK	General Department for Cooperation at the Ministry for Foreign Economic Relations
HEU	Highly Enriched Uranium
IAEA	International Atomic Energy Agency
ICBM	Intercontinental Ballistic Missiles
IMF	International Monetary Fund
MIRV	Multiple Independently Targetable Re-entry Vehicle
NAA	North Atlantic Assembly
NACC	North Atlantic Cooperation Council

NATO	North Atlantic Treaty Organization
NNA	Neutral and Non-Aligned (states)
NPT	Non-Proliferation Treaty
OECD	Organization for Economic Cooperation and Development
PFP	Partnership for Peace
SHAPE	Supreme Headquarters Allied Powers Europe
START	Strategic Arms Reduction Talks
SLBM	Submarine-launched Ballistic Missile
THAAD	Theatre High Altitude Air Defence
UNFICYP	United Nations Forces in Cyprus
UNIDIR	United Nations Institute for Disarmament
UNPROFOR	United Nations Protection Force
UNSC	United Nations Security Council
WEU	Western European Union

ACKNOWLEDGMENTS

The author is grateful to a broad range of people for help with this work. There have been many from the former Soviet Union and Eastern Europe who gave of their time and knowledge, and particular thanks are due to those from the British and other governments, the mass media and academic sector who provided helpful comments on earlier drafts in the study groups held in Chatham House. At different times, Neil Malcolm, Roy Allison, Professor Sir Laurence Martin and Neil Melvin were particular sources of helpful guidance within Chatham House, and Pavel Baev was also kind enough to send written comments from Norway on earlier drafts.

The Library staff at Chatham House provided their usual excellent support for this project and Emma Matanle, the International Security Programme Administrator in Chatham House, supplied valuable prompting, help and support to bring the text to its final form. Shyama Iyer helpfully typed later textual amendments. The author is very grateful to Margaret May and Hannah Doe for their high-quality, good-humoured and patient editorial work and for organizing the production process. The author must have responsibility for the shortcomings of the book, but would wish to ensure that any credit is shared.

June 1994   Trevor Taylor

1 INTRODUCTION

The concerns of the study

With the end of the Soviet Union, the West has now to deal with a series of dynamic new security issues while trying to tidy up the remnants of old concerns. Moreover, it must address them, not through a single government in Moscow with a clear source of effective authority, but through the 15 new governments of the successor states, in which the limits of the political power of any individual or section of government are often unclear.

This study is concerned with the big picture: with the policies the West needs to pursue to deal with the numerous security problems arising in the former Soviet Union (FSU), both potential and actual. To create a sense of perspective on issues of particular importance, the analysis pays special attention to the future impact of three factors which have been carried forward from the end of the Cold War – the role of the Commonwealth of Independent States (CIS) as a sort of successor entity to the Soviet Union, the importance of the Russian government, and the centrality of NATO in Western policies. Significantly, the number and diversity both of Western states and of successor states to the Soviet Union, and the range of different but interrelated security issues to be addressed, together mean that the maintenance of consistency and coherence among Western policies will be a major challenge.

This work was completed at a time of continuing rapid change in the former Soviet Union (FSU). With the ambitious aim of giving the text relevance for a period of years rather than months, the work, in so far as it refers to the past, includes events up to the spring of 1994.

However, in looking at the future, it seeks to discuss issues and responses in an analytical framework which, it is hoped, will have some durability: in particular, its scheme for classifying the security concerns resulting from the break-up of the Soviet Union should continue to have validity in the longer term. It seeks mainly to highlight the key desirable characteristics of Western policy, rather than focusing on specific policy recommendations. Since the most prudent and perhaps valid perspective on the FSU is that almost anything could happen – indeed one leading scholar has written that 'surprise remains one of the few things one can count on'[1] – Western policy needs a dual aspect. It needs to promote the most favourable developments that can be anticipated, and be prepared to counteract the effects of the worst.

Western policy practitioners and analysts also need to accept that, in the FSU, things are not always what they appear and not too much reliance can be placed on any single development or commitment. When, in the spring of 1994 Russia and Ukraine finally reached an agreement on the division of the Black Sea Fleet which was acceptable to the parliaments of both countries, it did not signify that the dispute was resolved, it merely meant that conflict was transferred to issues of where the fleet should be based. While Russia quite quickly agreed to withdraw its forces from Lithuania, friction remained because of disagreement about the transit rights across Lithuania which Russia claimed in order to bring forces to and from Kaliningrad. When Russia agreed in January 1994 to provide Ukraine with nuclear power station fuel in exchange for fissile material from missiles in Ukraine, there was subsequent uncertainty as to whether the Russian enterprise responsible for the fuel would in fact supply it to Ukraine unless the Russian government had paid all its outstanding debts to the firm.

This is related to two other difficulties faced by outside scholars of the FSU. One is that the FSU, having been a closed society about which information was scarce, has become much more open. On a large, socially and politically diverse region, there is now a vast amount of information available in the public sector, not least about the armed forces, but it is not always easy to judge its quality: thus official Russian data on economic performance fail to capture much private-sector activity. Government officials, as sometimes in the West, particularly highlight data which promote their interest of the moment so that, for instance, in the long discussions about the future of nuclear forces in Ukraine, there were many Russian statements about the deteriorating safety of the warheads and the missiles. These assessments were difficult to evaluate because they clearly served Russian purposes.

The second difficulty is that the new governments in the FSU, and especially the Russian government, are scarcely unitary, coherent actors. The announcement of a policy by the Russian president, for instance on export controls, far from guarantees its implementation. The gaps which have appeared and will appear between the Russian president, his foreign minister, the defence ministry, different sections of the armed forces, the parliament and so on are a constant challenge for the external analyst.

Before going further, however, some definitional points must be addressed: in particular, what is meant by 'security' problems and 'the West'.

The nature of security issues

Traditionally, security issues in international politics have been seen as those which relate in one way or another to the threat, use or control of armed force. A major debate is under way in the West about the bases and nature of security on the global scale, in which those supporting the traditional line clash with others who perceive the most serious threats to people's lives as mostly non-military in nature and so not subject to military solutions.[2]

This study both espouses the traditional argument, with its stress on the centrality of military force (and forces as organizations) in the security sphere, and adopts a broad approach. The core of concern is the place which the threat and use of force will play in the international relations linking the new states of the former Soviet Union with one another and with the West. The determinants of such relations will, however, encompass a wide range of economic and political factors, as well as the distribution of military power among states. The place of armed force in international political relations will also be influenced by the size, structure, doctrinal orientations and equipment of the militaries in the successor states and in those of their neighbours. In this approach, an environmental problem is not a security issue unless it contributes (as it well might) to the serious deterioration of political relations among two or more states. Similarly, factors such as the changing role of religion, economic progress or deprivation, currency stability, migratory movements and so on could eventually have an impact in the security sector, but have, by and large, been regarded as beyond the scope of this work. The emphasis here is on what the security-defence sector of Western governments can do, while recognizing that it is unable to promote stable and cooperative security relations in isolation from the rest of Western governmental machinery.

'The West' and other groupings

Some brief words are needed also about 'the West'. During most of the Cold War, NATO states comprised the core of this concept, with Europe's neutral and non-aligned (NNA) states sharing many of the values and aspirations of the NATO countries. There were always issues at the margins: in particular could Australia and New Zealand, geographically distant but with much in common culturally, economically and politically with Western Europe and the US, be considered part of the West? Also, by the end of the Cold War, a further issue was the sense in which Japan also comprised part of the West: its commitment to democracy, a free society and a market economy associated it closely with Western values, and its economic activities and strength tied it to Western economic concerns, as its membership of the original G5 (later G7) and the Organization for Economic Cooperation and Development (OECD) made clear. Western Europe and Japan are linked by many common security concerns,[3] which have led to a growing Japanese interest in NATO and the Conference on Security and Cooperation in Europe (CSCE), but in many ways Japan is in a very different security situation to the countries of NATO. This study therefore does not treat Japan as part of the West but it does recognize the significance and weight of Tokyo. There are a number of security questions involving the FSU where North America and Western Europe would benefit from Japan's participation in their policies.

In addition, this work does not yet treat any of the former communist countries of Europe as part of the West, despite their growing links with such Western bodies as NATO and the European Union (EU). Their ties are not yet sufficiently deep and varied and their political situation is still special. Table 1 gives a digest of how 'the West' and some other terms are used here. Significantly, only one term, Western Europe, is defined in terms of institutional membership, and even that constitutes a contentious case.

Structure

The overall structure of the book is as follows. Chapters 2 to 4 seek to build on definitional points to catalogue the many security-related issues in the FSU that have become apparent since the period 1990–91. They classify into three categories the most telling factors which relate clearly to the military sector. The first category, addressed in Chapter 2, includes those elements of capability which mean that the states in the FSU retain a military potential to attack the West directly or, through proliferation processes, to strengthen other states which might be inclined to threaten the West. Into the second category, covered in Chapter 3, fall those economic and political problems arising in the FSU as a result of past and continuing military efforts: for instance, the size and weight of the armed forces in the successor states of the FSU have many problematic features and their establishment, reduction and restructuring present many difficulties. The third category, considered in Chapter 4, comprises those political issues, of borders, ethnic rights and government, which the parties in the FSU may seek or are seeking to resolve by force.

Table 1: Working definitions of regions

Term	Definition	Notes/qualifications
The West	Members of NATO plus Europe's neutral and non-aligned (NNA) states	(excluding Albania and the successor states of the former NNA state of Yugoslavia)
Western Europe	Members of the European Union	Members of European Community after Maastricht form the EU, which also covers the Western European Union, with its similar membership. States in the geographical area of Western Europe not in the EU do not seek to generate a common foreign and security policy, as EU states do.
Europe	The countries comprising the West, less the US and Canada, plus the European NNAs including the successor states of the former Yugoslavia and Albania, plus Russia, Belarus, Ukraine, Georgia, Moldova, Estonia, Latvia and Lithuania, plus Poland, Hungary, the Czech Republic, the Slovak Republic, Bulgaria and Romania.	Countries comprising territories in the geographic areas of Asia and Europe (chiefly Russia and Turkey) are nonetheless included as part of Europe.
Central Europe	Poland, Hungary, the Czech Republic, the Slovak Republic.	
East/Central Europe	Estonia, Latvia, Lithuania, Poland, Hungary, the Czech Republic, the Slovak Republic, Bulgaria, Romania, Albania plus the successor states of the former Yugoslavia.	

Chapter 5 analyses the nature of Western interests in these areas, notes Western policy to date and suggests directions and priorities for action. Because Western security policy both in the past and the future involves extensive use of multilateral forums and international organizations, Chapter 6 analyses the institutional implications of the security issues in the FSU and Western reactions to them.

While this structure has the disadvantage of some inevitable repetition, it does mean that there is appropriate emphasis in the earlier chapters on the full extent of the daunting and varied security issues raised by the collapse of the USSR and the uncertainties of the continuing, comprehensive transformation of its successor states.

2 FSU SECURITY RISKS: PROLIFERATION AND DIRECT MILITARY THREATS

The direct dangers

After 1988, the direct threat of Soviet forces was much reduced by the troop withdrawals made by Moscow from the Czech and Slovak republics and Hungary; a timetable was also agreed with Germany for complete withdrawal by the end of 1994. After the failure of the August 1991 coup in Moscow, an agreement was concluded with Warsaw that the withdrawal of Soviet troops from Poland would be accelerated.[1] The timetable for withdrawal from Germany was also slightly speeded up.

With the break-up of the Soviet Union in 1992, Russia inherited the command and organizational structures (and many of the conventional forces) of the Soviet army. Led by Ukraine, Azerbaijan and Moldova, other successor states began establishing their own armed forces, sometimes using former Soviet units based on their soil. For some states progress was slow and the Belarus forces are being closely linked with those of Russia. An essential point in 1994 is that only Russia has conventional forces which could in theory eventually threaten the heartland of the West. However, given the collapse of the Warsaw Treaty Organization, the disruption of Russian defence production and the disarray in conscription arrangements, such a threat seems more remote than ever. From the end of 1994 a Russian army will have to cross Belarus, Ukraine and Poland before it can reach the West (a position which offers few chances for a surprise attack despite the 40,000 Russian troops still based in Belarus). One Ukrainian author has written, with some but not complete justification, that 'The Soviet threat to the West, which existed for over seven decades, was removed at one stroke by the December 1991 vote by Ukraine for independence'.[2] However, NATO has members (Norway and Turkey) which still share a common border with FSU states. Norway in particular is concerned about forces in the Kola peninsula, and over time Russia's capabilities will be shaped in part by its military ambitions.

The draft Russian military doctrine announced in May 1992 reflected the capabilities which the then Russian armed forces leadership would like to have and which, if implemented, could be viewed as dangerous for the West. The draft doctrine described two possible direct threats to Russia: the introduction of foreign troops in contiguous states, and the build-up of (neighbouring) forces near Russia's borders. However, 'in addition, a violation of the rights of Russian citizens and of persons "ethnically and culturally" identified with Russia in the former Soviet republics was viewed "as a serious source of conflicts"'.[3] More or less the whole Russian political spectrum has accepted that Russian 'fundamental national security interests' include 'defending the rights of Russians abroad'.[4] The head of the General Staff Academy, Colonel-General I. Rodionov, argued openly that Russia's 'vital interests' included at least the neutrality of the East European states which border on the Commonwealth of Independent States (CIS). He included also the Baltic states and the whole CIS as vital Russian interests and stressed the continued threat posed by the US and the West.[5] In the draft doctrine, while local conflicts were seen as the most likely to entail involvement of Russian forces, large-scale warfare could not be ruled out completely, and Defence Minister Grachev hinted at dissatisfaction with the Conventional Forces in Europe (CFE) Treaty limits because of the need to store equipment in Siberia. His clear implication was that the CFE Treaty did not give Russia enough equipment west of the Urals for its military needs.[6]

Clearly, many senior officers had been markedly impressed by the coalition performance in the war against Iraq and stressed Russia's need for accurate deep-strike weapons against the heart of the enemy, for the capacity to seize the initiative early on in the air and at sea, and for highly mobile ground forces with sophisticated command and control arrangements. Given that Belarus was the manufacturing (but not design) base of the Soviet military electronics industry, the implications were substantial for its continued independence. While in some ways the Russian military seem to have learned too much from the Kuwait campaign, and while the three types of force which Russia planned to develop looked suspiciously like an imitation of NATO thinking by people who had lost their own framework for thought, there were signs that important elements in Russia had not broken from old attitudes.[7] Consider the following statements from Defence Minister Grachev: his argument that 'preventing a war is the basic political objective of the state' can be used to justify the militarization of society; his assertions that 'we should not allow ourselves to lag behind a probable enemy as regards preparing the armed forces and mobilizing the economy for the commencement of hostilities. We must not forget the lessons of 1941' raise questions as to which 'probable enemy' he has in mind. He recognized that Russian military doctrine should be 'a corollary to the overall basic concept of Russia's security, formulating the goals and tasks of the state's policy and determining the priority interests of the Russian Federation. Furthermore it should also express our state's attitude towards the use of military force to attain political ends'.[8] Yet there was no readiness to grant civilian foreign policy authorities a major role in developing military doctrine. Overall General Grachev gave 'the impression of being a plain-speaking traditionalist who is committed to having powerful armed forces enabling Russia to act from a position of strength on the international stage'.[9]

The three types of Russian forces were to be: ready, forward-deployed forces able to repel local aggression; rapid-response, mobile forces which could quickly be deployed to any region to repel more serious aggression; and strategic reserves assembled in the threat period or war itself to conduct large-scale combat operations.

By 1992, the consensus of military thinking was that Russian force capabilities should reflect 'defensive sufficiency', rather than the 'reasonable sufficiency' criterion which had prevailed under Gorbachev; pre-emptive strikes had come into consideration, and some senior soldiers stressed the need to be able to defeat rather than just repel the enemy. For many military thinkers, the first use of nuclear weapons could be contemplated. The draft doctrine itself appeared contradictory, stating on the one hand that Russia pledged never to initiate the use of nuclear weapons, and on the other that if an aggressor undertook 'actions involving the purposeful disruption of strategic nuclear forces and the destruction of nuclear power and other potentially dangerous installations, even by conventional means, this would be taken as a transition to the use of weapons of mass destruction'.[10] A limited nuclear war was seen once more as feasible; whereas in 1990 its consequences were held to be certainly catastrophic, in 1992 the term used was 'might' be catastrophic.

The contrast of all this both with President Yeltsin's assertion that Russia would not be the first to use nuclear or other weapons of mass destruction, and with the view of a prominent Russian arms control official that 'the greatest real security risk to Russia in the years to come would be the continuation of the relentless arms race, which has already resulted in the country's near economic collapse',[11] was striking and pointed to areas of friction between the civil section of the government and senior military figures. A British authority, noting the draft doctrine's lack of attention to crisis management or war termination, and its implicit assumption of hostility towards Russia on the part of the US and NATO, observed that 'in some respects, the new draft doctrine is even more reactionary and even more divorced from (apparent) government policy' than the 1990 version.[12]

The May 1992 draft was never submitted for legal approval by parliament, if only because it was written on the (bizarre) assumption that the CIS would be an effective, working alliance. But it should not be ignored given its reflection of General Staff thought. From late 1992 stress on the importance of the near abroad increased.[13] The Russian Foreign Ministry published on 1 December 1992 a foreign policy concept which stressed the significance and sensitivity of Russia's near abroad, Russia in the first six months of its independent existence having tended to neglect the other successor states and then to place too much emphasis on the potential of the CIS.[14] While the formal status of this concept remained unclear,[15] its emphasis was unambiguous:

> The most important foreign policy tasks, requiring the coordinated and constant efforts of all state structures, are the cessation and regulation of all conflicts around Russia, the inadmissibility of their spreading on our territory, and the provision of strict observation in the near abroad of human and minority rights, particularly of Russians and the Russian speaking population.[16]

The concept also argued firmly for the need to defend the external borders of the CIS, so as better to protect Russia against crime, drugs and arms smuggling. The interventionist powers which Russia implied it could claim were apparent. In July 1993 President Yeltsin reportedly chided the chiefs of the army in the Russian Security Council for not better protecting the Tajikistan–Afghan borders where 25 Russian border guards had been recently killed.[17] Russia's formal position on intervention remains that it does not need the permission of the UN or the CSCE to send 'peace-making' forces to CIS states but that in all cases it sends troops only 'in reply to the requests and with the consent of corresponding states and conflicting sides'.[18]

When a final version of Russia's military doctrine was approved by President Yeltsin in November 1993, some elements in the previous General Staff draft had disappeared, but not quite all of the 23 pages of the doctrine were released. The doctrine stressed the desirability of the abolition of all weapons of mass destruction and underlined Russia's commitment to the Biological and Chemical Weapons Convention, but it also reserved Russia's right to use nuclear weapons against any state attacking it. This seemed to reflect a lack of confidence over the long term in Russia's capacity to produce state-of-the-art conventional weapons and effective conventional forces. The doctrine listed 10 principal and existing sources of external military danger including 'existing and potential areas of local wars ... especially near Russia's frontiers', 'suppression of the rights, freedom and lawful interests of

Russian citizens in foreign states', attacks on Russian military facilities located in foreign states, and 'expansion of military blocs and alliances to the detriment of Russian military security'. It also categorized eight internal sources of military threat, including attacks on nuclear installations and organized crime.

There was much that the West could find encouraging: 'Measures to ensure the security of the RF [Russian Federation] must not be at the expense of others' security ... International obligations must be observed ... Arms control will be pursued'; the US and NATO were no longer defined as the enemies of Russia. But Russia also asserted a right to maintain 'stability' in the regions surrounding it. In line with the 1992 draft, the doctrine stressed commitment to appropriate defence spending and to the defence industries.[19]

In terms of whether and how Russia should be viewed as a direct threat to the West, the draft and approved military doctrines had an ambiguous flavour. Encouragingly, it was clear that Russia was drawn increasingly to concentrating its military attention on the 'near abroad' rather than on NATO states, and that the final military doctrine had been developed in a specific, civilian foreign policy context. But the term 'near abroad' included a degree of geographical ambiguity: in particular it was uncertain if it included the Baltic states, although Defence Minister Grachev on a visit to Switzerland in late 1993 said that the Baltics were not part of the near abroad.[20] When in the spring of 1994 President Yeltsin signed a decree for the establishment of Russian military bases around the FSU, it took some time to clarify that these would not involve the Baltic states[21] (with the agreed exception of the Skrunda facility in Latvia – see below). The Baltic states clearly were not subject to any formal Western security guarantee but it would be difficult for NATO simply to accept their intimidation by the Russian military, not least because the West had never accepted that these countries were legally part of the Soviet Union and the independence of the Baltic states also had strong support from the north European members of NATO. In addition there were fears about an apparent continuing Russian ambition for military might; it was thought that if

Russia succeeded in re-establishing domination over the near abroad, it might then return to seeking hegemony over East/Central Europe. This thought sharpened the issues for the West of whether, when and how it should extend security guarantees, including NATO membership, to the Central European countries. What price should NATO pay to prevent an intimidatory Moscow from re-establishing a military position in Central Europe?

At the nuclear level, Russia clearly maintained a substantial strategic capability which could be used against the West. In 1992 the former Soviet forces were given a CIS character under the military command of Air Force Marshal Yevgeny Shaposhnikov, but political control was vested solely in the Russian President. In the summer of 1993 even the image of a CIS command was abandoned, when Russia accepted that it needed national armed forces and Marshal Shaposhnikov moved to head Russia's Security Council.[22] Even when the START 2 Treaty is implemented Russia will have more than 3,000 strategic warheads at its disposal, but implementation of that agreement could well be delayed. However, all former Soviet tactical nuclear weapons have been withdrawn from all the FSU successor states into Russia and, apart from the air-launched weapons, presumably taken out of service. It is hard to envisage political circumstances in which nuclear intimidation by Russia in isolation from conventional forces would appear a realistic option against the West.

There is a further danger which relates to former Soviet nuclear forces but which would not involve their deliberate political or military use by the Russian state (or the CIS) against the West. This is that a small, desperate, even insane element in the CIS armed forces might try to cause chaos by launching a strategic nuclear weapon without central political authorization. Some reports indicated that 'Gorbachev or other political authorities probably cannot prevent the senior military commanders from exercising effective military control over nuclear weapons in a leadership crisis, or from launching them ... Gorbachev's [nuclear button] is probably neither necessary nor sufficient to initiate a Soviet nuclear attack'.[23] Yet formal responsibility for a launch of such weapons, and with it the 'nuclear football' with nuclear release codes, clearly passed from President Gorbachev of the USSR to President Yeltsin of Russia when Gorbachev resigned in December 1991, and senior Russian military officers have repeatedly stressed that nuclear forces are under effective control. The situation was reassessed in 1993 in a major study by Bruce Blair in which he stressed the Russian obsession with control over nuclear weapons. The arrangements for the command and control of strategic nuclear forces in the FSU appeared as effective in 1994 as they were in 1987 and yet in March 1994 there was an alarming breakdown of order when a Russian soldier, apparently a mentally deranged recruit from Dagestan, went on the rampage at a nuclear missile installation in southwestern Siberia and killed several people. As sources from Russia admit, there were real fears that a bullet hitting a missile could have ignited the fuel.[24] The incident revealed the difficulties of maintaining the quality of strategic missile forces at a time when armed forces leaders were all too aware of the low standards in terms of fitness, intelligence and integrity of many conscripts.

In principle Russian nuclear command and control could deteriorate rapidly in the event of civil war, but here Blair is quite optimistic. 'In my estimation, the regime of existing safeguards, combined with the command system's adaptive capacity, should inspire confidence in the system's ability to endure acute domestic turmoil probably on a scale far exceeding anything witnessed to date and to contain the effects of aberrant behaviour within the nuclear chain of command and throughout the life of the nuclear weapons'.[25] The conclusion must be that the serious nature of any loss of Russian central control over nuclear weapons must make it a concern for the West, but that in 1994 the situation is still far from alarming. The complete professionalization of the strategic missile forces would be a source of relief for the West.

A different sort of nuclear danger could arise from the physical deterioration of weapons, which could lead to radiation releases affecting the West or more likely East/Central Europe. Western visitors to storage sites have not been impressed by the physical arrangements for the safe storage of weapons and at least one Russian nuclear expert has anticipated major problems as weapons are dismantled. Boris Gorbachev, a leading weapons designer, asserted that gas will build up to dangerous levels within warheads, that older weapons have problematic detonators, that there will be insufficient experts to dismantle weapons, and that explosions spreading radioactive material will occur.[26] The Russian army's General Mikhail Kolesnikov said in March 1993 that strategic warheads in Ukraine were leaking dangerous amounts of radiation because Russian authorities could not maintain the missiles.[27] This was only one of many Russian reports of the dangers of leaving weapons in Ukraine. Such assertions cannot be dismissed entirely as exaggerations designed to pressure Ukraine and the other republics with nuclear weapons on their soil to give up those warheads, or as scare-mongering to secure Western aid for the former Soviet nuclear scientific community. It is important to note that these problems will have a long-term character.

Overall, the immediate direct military threat (an amalgam of capability and intention) against the West from Russia and the CIS was minimal even by the middle of 1992. This clearly does not negate the possibility that Russia and/or the CIS might change course and try once more to dominate through military means the states of Central Europe or the Baltic for which the West does not (yet) have any direct security responsibility. Moreover, after change, reorganization and growth, the Russian Federation might in a couple of decades once more become a great military power which tries to take over its neighbours. However, this would require considerable economic and military strength, the prospects for which do not seem good. The evidence of the past 50 years is that Russia has considerable economic potential, but to exploit it will require a drastic reduction in its military effort, as is discussed in Chapter 3.

The indirect threat: proliferation

Nuclear proliferation within the CIS appears particularly as a threat to relations within the former Soviet empire, but its wider consequences for the West would be very negative. Should either Ukraine, Belarus or Kazakhstan aim firmly at recognition as a nuclear power, it would poison relations within the FSU and make the reinforcement of the global non-proliferation regime at the nuclear Non-Proliferation Treaty (NPT) conference in 1995 much more problematic.[28]

The starting-point for analysis must be that, when the Soviet Union broke up, tactical nuclear weapons were located in (probably) all of the constituent republics. Strategic nuclear weapons were based in Belarus, Kazakhstan and Ukraine, in addition to Russia. Table 2 gives the detail.

After the break-up of the USSR there was a confusing and occasionally contradictory series of statements, political commitments and legal undertakings.

(1) In December 1991, at the Alma Ata CIS summit, all the CIS states agreed to allow the return to Russia by July 1992 of all tactical nuclear weapons on their territory.

(2) At the CIS Minsk meeting on 14 February 1992, the CIS members agreed to keep all strategic nuclear forces under a single CIS command,[29] with Moscow's plan being to remove all intercontinental ballistic missiles (ICBMs) from Ukraine by 1994 and from Belarus and Kazakhstan by 1998.[30]

(3) In March 1992 Ukraine briefly halted the return of tactical weapons to Russia, apparently on the grounds that the weapons would not be destroyed and might in future be used to Russia's advantage against Ukraine.[31]

(4) In Lisbon on 23 May 1992, Ukraine, Belarus and Kazakhstan signed with Russia and the US a Protocol to the START 1 Treaty under which they agreed to take on the obligations of the USSR. Ukraine, Belarus and Kazakhstan had said previously that they did not want to be nuclear weapon states,[32] and they agreed in Lisbon that all nuclear forces would be removed from their territory within seven years. They also agreed that they would sign the Non-Proliferation Treaty (NPT) as non-nuclear weapon states in the shortest possible time. President Kravchuk of

Table 2: CIS strategic nuclear forces outside Russia

	Ukraine	Belarus	Kazakhstan
SS.18 Site(s)			104 Derzhavinsk & Zhangiz-Tobe
SS.19 Site(s)	130 Pervomaysk & Khmel'Nitskiy		
SS.24 Site(s)	46 Pervomaysk		
SS.25 Site(s)		c.80 Lida & Mozyr	
TU.95H6/H16 Bear Site	22 Uzin		40 Semipalatinsk
TU.160 Blackjack Site	20 Priluki		

Source: IISS, *The Military Balance 1992–3*, London, 1992.

Ukraine asserted the value of a nuclear-free zone in the Black Sea region.[33] The cuts involved in the START Treaty of July 1991 did not directly necessitate the destruction of those weapons based outside Russia, although the USSR was obliged to destroy half its total of 354 SS.18s. The START Treaty did, however, bar its signatories from stationing weapons in other states; this meant that Russian weapons could not be kept in other successor republics.[34]

(5) In June 1992 Presidents Bush and Yeltsin agreed on two further stages of strategic arms cuts. By the end of the second stage, among other changes, all MIRVed ICBMs would be abandoned. The SS.18s, 19s and 24s with their multiple warheads would

have to disappear from the Russian/CIS arsenal. This agreement
was turned into a legal commitment, the START 2 Treaty, at
the beginning of 1993. By February 1993 Belarus, Kazakhstan
and Russia had ratified the START 1 Treaty, although Ukraine
had not, and neither Belarus, Kazakhstan nor Ukraine had signed
the NPT.[35] Russia had made it clear that for Moscow imple-
menting START 2 would depend on the three other republics
signing the NPT.

In 1992 Belarus expected its mobile SS.25s to be withdrawn and that
strategic nuclear aircraft would be removed to Russia and/or destroyed.[36] In 1994 its defence minister confirmed that the withdrawal
of weapons was on schedule and could well be concluded before the
target date of 1999.[37] Belarus should, in fact, be free of nuclear weapons
in fact by mid-1996. In contrast Ukraine adopted a complex and
perhaps dangerous approach. One element in Ukrainian thinking was
economic. Ukraine wanted to be compensated in full for any costs it
incurred in the removal and dismantling of the missiles and to receive
its share of revenue from any sale to the West of surplus fissile material
by Russia. Also, elements in Ukraine's political elite indicated that
Ukraine might want to obtain full control of the 46 SS.24 ICBMs
positioned in Ukraine and not scheduled to be destroyed under the
START 1 Treaty, although they were less concerned about the 130
other ICBMs in Ukraine which would be destroyed when START 1
was implemented.[38] In a UN publication prepared during the spring of
1992, Victor Batiouk, a Ukrainian foreign service officer, explained his
view of his government's position and, in doing so, implicitly exposed
some problem areas. Thus he noted that under the May 1992 Lisbon
protocol to the START 1 Treaty, Belarus, Kazakhstan and Ukraine
agreed to *destroy or turn over* to Russia all strategic warheads.[39] But then
he also wrote of 'the solemn Ukrainian promise that no removal of
nuclear armaments for redeployment in Russia would take place'.[40] It
is on these grounds that Ukraine would not allow the strategic bombers
on Ukrainian territory to fly to Russia with their weapons (although

Ukraine had allowed the removal of tactical weapons without being able to verify their destruction). Despite its agreement in May, Ukraine was unwilling to 'turn over' strategic weapons to Russia: since the CIS was not seen as being in a position to destroy weapons on a collective, cooperative basis, Ukraine itself wanted to destroy the nuclear weapons on its territory, and to receive significant Western financial help for so doing.

Command and control of the weapons was itself problematic. One Ukrainian theme was the state's desire, even capability, to prevent the use of the weapons. As the Ukrainian parliament declared in October 1991, 'Ukraine insists on its right to control the non-use of nuclear weapons located within its territory'.[41] Ukraine also asserted responsibility for the physical safety of the weapons and talked of having administrative control over them. Yet elsewhere it also acknowledged that the strategic forces in Ukraine are 'part and parcel of the joint strategic forces of the Commonwealth of Independent States and control over them is exercised by Russia's President Boris Yeltsin', who is merely obliged to consult with the President of Ukraine before their use.[42]

Linked to these issues was the question of ownership. By the beginning of 1993 Kazakhstan and Belarus appeared content with *de facto* Russian ownership and control,[43] but the predominant impression from Ukrainian statements was that nuclear weapons were no exception to the rule that 'everything that is situated on Ukrainian territory belongs to Ukraine in the same way that whatever is on Russian territory belongs to Russia'.[44] If and when all nuclear weapons in Ukraine disappeared and Ukraine signed the Non-Proliferation Treaty, it saw itself doing so as a nuclear power which had consciously opted to abandon this status. It did not see itself as a power like Germany during the Cold War, which had nuclear weapons on its territory and available in some circumstances to German forces, but which was not itself a nuclear weapons state. Ukraine justified this in part through the involvement of its citizens in former Soviet nuclear programmes.[45] By arranging the Lisbon protocol, the US appeared to have accepted this

Ukrainian view, which may make it difficult in future to produce effective Western reasoning should Ukraine decide to reverse its eventual January 1994 commitments to give up 'its' nuclear weapons and to accede to the NPT as a non-nuclear weapon state.

Some feeling in Ukraine was profoundly anti-nuclear, not least because of the horrors of the Chernobyl experience, and clear arguments could be articulated that Ukrainian nuclear forces would help neither its security nor its economy. But opposition to giving up nuclear forces could also be closely tied to strong anti-Russian, anti-Western and pro-nationalist feelings, which hinted that Ukraine should be ready to renounce 'its' nuclear forces only when the US and Russia were ready to give up theirs.[46] Those arguing this line seemed to believe that nuclear weapons could somehow help Ukraine in its political relations with Moscow, including disputes over Crimea, the Black Sea Fleet and Sevastopol. Overall, Ukraine's reluctance to forsake nuclear weapons reflected the difficult state of its political relations with Moscow.

These were serious developments, which raised important questions. Could Ukraine or any of the other states concerned prevent the launch of strategic forces in defiance of an order from Moscow? Ukraine after all had a stance of non-alignment and 'in case of war will remain neutral (unless it is attacked)'.[47] Could Ukrainian forces seize the weapons? Could the Ukraine government defeat the code locks on the weapons and fire them against Moscow's will? Could Ukraine re-target the missiles and, if so, with what degree of accuracy? Which of the three republics could effectively maintain the missiles and their warheads? There were no clear answers to any of these questions,[48] although few doubted Ukraine's eventual capability to defeat the code locks. (Blair observed that it would be uncharacteristic if the Russian command system had not prepared contingency plans for the emergency disabling and recovery of strategic nuclear weapons to foil any attempt by an emboldened state like Ukraine to seize them by force.[49]) The position of the bombers was curious since the Ukrainian parliament apparently showed little interest in them,[50] yet they could have been used against Russia more easily than the missiles.[51] Like the missiles, however, they were very vulnerable to a Russian first strike and Russia could well have stored the bombs well away from the aircraft. Some felt that Ukraine's control over the bombers might have been quite comprehensive,[52] but it is also possible that Russia secretly dismantled and/or flew out the bombs formerly based in Ukraine.

These significant issues were and remain of great concern to the West, although the nuclear thinking of Ukraine and Kazakhstan indicated that it was not the West about which they were particularly worried. Fear of nuclear (and/or conventional) military intimidation efforts from Moscow played a role and it was also likely that Ukraine was trying to use its hold on nuclear forces (and its claims on the Black Sea Fleet) as bargaining chips in its effort to get Moscow to accept that Crimea should remain part of Ukraine.

Kazakhstan has no anti-Russian political stance but it does have concern about potential Russian and Chinese claims on its territory.[53] Clearly, the possibility could not be entirely discounted that, with a different government, Kazakhstan would in time become profoundly Islamic and anti-Russian in its political identification, involving the alienation of the significant Russian elements in the population. However, Iran is currently not encouraging fundamentalism in the area and in 1994 President Nazarbayev is working for a cooperative relationship with Russia and apparently has seen the nuclear weapons on his territory as bargaining counters in his wider relationship with Moscow and the West. Thus when he visited Moscow in the spring of 1994 he encouraged Russia to provide a friendly reception by announcing Kazakhstan's ratification of the NPT. Ukraine (repeatedly) and Kazakhstan both expressed interest in being given positive Western security guarantees, stronger than those provided to non-nuclear states under the UN Security Council commitments which *de facto* form a part of the Non-Proliferation Treaty regime. Ukraine in fact sought guarantees against nuclear and conventional threats, as well as economic warfare, and seemingly wanted Moscow to guarantee continued energy supplies at favourable prices.

During 1993, however, Ukraine seemed gradually to abandon its immediate nuclear ambitions in the face of a worsening economic situation, deterioration in the condition of missiles (especially the SS.24s) and warheads on its soil, and Western pressure. While the two separate deals in the summer and early autumn of 1993 between Presidents Kravchuk and Yeltsin (reached in Moscow and Massandra respectively) on Ukrainian nuclear disarmament and the division of the Black Sea Fleet failed in the face of parliamentary criticism, the January 1994 agreement by Yeltsin, Kravchuk and Clinton was endorsed by the Ukrainian parliament, which also abandoned the 13 conditions it had set in the autumn of 1993 for the ratification of the START 1 Treaty.[54] Under the January agreement Ukraine, Russia and the US agreed that the strategic warheads in Ukraine would be returned as soon as possible to Russia for dismantling. The highly enriched uranium (HEU) in the warheads would be reprocessed and the equivalent amount of nuclear fuel delivered simultaneously to Ukraine. Similar exchange arrangements were planned for HEU from Belarus and Kazakhstan. The missiles would be dismantled and the US later agreed to provide $700 million to fund this operation, with Japan also being ready to make a contribution.[55] Russia and the US agreed to provide Ukraine with various security assurances, including both negative and positive assurances about the threat of nuclear weapons, once the START 1 Treaty came into force and Ukraine acceded to the NPT as a non-nuclear weapon state.[56] The first trainload of warheads quickly left Ukraine.[57]

The agreement could be seen as a triumph for Ukraine, especially since the envisaged security assurances included an agreement to 'refrain from economic coercion'. However, the agreement will take some years to implement in full and Ukrainian government attitudes could change again, especially after the presidential elections in summer 1994. Even by early February there was some friction over Russian allegations that Ukraine was still seeking to gain practical control over the weapons, despite the January agreement's provision that Ukraine would help Russia to maintain the warheads in a safe condition prior to their removal to Russia.[58] By April Ukraine was asking Russia to forgive more than three times as much in Ukrainian debts as Russia was willing to consider (700 billion roubles as opposed to 200 billion) as compensation for the return of strategic bombers. Ukraine also complained that Russia was not delivering on time the nuclear fuel to which it was committed (perhaps because the Russian enterprise supplying the fuel had not itself been paid by the Russian government).[59] The Ukrainian defence minister, on a visit to Germany, hinted that Ukraine might halt its nuclear disarmament process. Given that the Russian-Ukraine argument over the Black Sea Fleet and its bases was also being waged fiercely in the spring of 1994 and that Ukraine will not acquire the security assurances until it has ratified the NPT, a measure it had not taken by the late spring of 1994, the Ukrainian nuclear issue will need continuous monitoring.

Ukraine clearly expected its January commitment to nuclear disarmament to bring further Western economic aid and support in general. Kravchuk claimed to have won a promise which would double US annual economic aid to Ukraine to $350 million during his visit to Washington in March 1994. Thus keeping Ukraine on the de-nuclearizing path could well mean the West's providing appropriate economic incentives. Kazakhstan, too, may try to increase the benefits it receives for actual nuclear disarmament now it has seen what Ukraine could obtain in the way of security guarantees.[60] However, the last nuclear-capable aircraft had gone back to Russia from Kazakhstan by March 1994[61] (without Kazakhstan being paid for it) and, as noted, Kazakhstan ratified the NPT in early 1994.

A further danger, or rather set of proliferation dangers, is that control might simply be lost over some of the 9,000–28,000[62] tactical nuclear weapons in Russia, resulting in their export. Uncertainties about just how many weapons there are reflect doubts about the number of (mainly old) weapons which were in storage as opposed to being deployed with forces. One authoritative (private) UK estimate was that the FSU in 1993 had about 30,000 nuclear warheads in all, of which 11–13,000 could be counted as 'strategic', the balance being 'tactical'.

In principle, some of these weapons could be illicitly sold to those, perhaps Middle East-based, terrorists who want a nuclear capability to use against the West. While Russian military leaders have repeatedly reassured the West that this will not happen because of the discipline and procedures of the Russian troops which control such weapons, the possibility cannot be discounted, especially if Russia descends into civil war and chaos. Although the US and Russia have agreed that most non-strategic nuclear weapons should be destroyed, it will take at least a decade to dismantle even a majority of the Soviet systems, and even then there will be a problem of taking care of weapons-grade pluto-nium, highly enriched uranium and other radioactive and sensitive materials.[63] US sources found that there are six sites in Russia where fissionable materials sufficient for at least one weapon are stored, none of them covered by IAEA safeguards. In addition, Belarus and Kazakhstan each have one such site.[64] Russia's 1994 agreement to cease production of specialized weapons-grade plutonium by the end of the year should prevent this significant problem becoming even bigger.[65] Moreover, illegally acquired tactical weapons, probably well beyond their 'sell-by' date, would appeal most obviously to desperate groups, perhaps terrorists, who were willing to make use of essentially unreliable systems.

The long-term significance of Russia's nuclear stockpile cannot easily be understated. A crucial technical consideration is that not only must Russia's nuclear weapons be kept in safe and secure storage, it is also necessary on a more or less permanent basis to look after the fissile materials (plutonium and highly enriched uranium) taken from disassem-bled weapons. In the global effort to control nuclear proliferation, restricting the supply of the fissile material – which is difficult to manufacture – is of crucial importance, since knowledge of how to manufacture nuclear weapons as such is relatively widespread. Russia has hundreds of tons of such materials to protect, and there are no easy ways of rendering them into substances useless for military purposes. The West is right to recognize that Russia's nuclear weapons arsenal makes it a country of special importance in the former Soviet empire, and thus requiring special treatment. However, in many ways it is Moscow's redundant weapons stock rather than its active forces that causes the greatest concern for the West, indeed for those sectors of the international community as a whole which oppose further nuclear proliferation.

Russia also has an extensive stock of chemical weapons (it admits to 40,000 tons[66]) which could in principle find their way abroad, as well as acknowledged (and illegal) biological warfare technology. The poor condition of many of the chemical weapons makes it unlikely that they would be stolen or sold illicitly. Although predictably Russia has a full plan for dealing with its chemical weapons,[67] the biggest problem is likely to be funding the cost of their destruction under the Chemical Weapons Convention (CWC), probably on the sites where they are presently stored. The cost of destroying stored weapons will not be modest: Russia is thinking of around 2,000 billion roubles at 1993 prices while US estimates are of a sum around $9 billion.[68] It seems unlikely that the Russian parliament will ratify the CWC without assurances of at least $500 million in Western help, and weapons destruction will not be easy, not least because of the fears of residents near storage-destruction sites. In addition, the difficulty and cost of cleaning up sites of already dumped weapons is likely to be even greater. Some weapons were dumped during the Second World War, for instance in the Baltic, the Arctic and the Black Sea,[69] and the strong financial temptation will be to leave dumped weapons in the sea where they lie in the hope that they do not cause an environmental catastrophe in the future.[70]

The biological weapons position must be a source of concern to the West, given that such technology is so easy to hide and that Russia has admitted that it had an active research programme until the early 1990s. In 1994 it denies that it either develops or produces biological weapons, although there are rumours to the contrary.[71] The Soviet Union formally signed and ratified the Biological Weapons Convention and Russia inherited its commitment. The West needs to worry about proliferation as a result of the possible leaking of earlier biological weapons technology development from Russia and about the direct threat to the West such weapons could pose should Russia's political orientation become hostile. However, the political circumstances under which Russia could threaten or use biological warfare are not easy to imagine outside the context of a large-scale war against a Western state or coalition. It is a source of some reassurance for the West that Russia is being more open about its past activities in this area. A significant Anglo-American visit to Moscow took place in September 1992 to discuss compliance with the Biological Weapons Convention; this was followed by a Western visit to the suspect Ultrapure Biological Preparations plant in St Petersburg. In late 1992 Moscow introduced particular regulations to control the export of agents which could be used in biological weapons,[72] but there must be questions about the effectiveness with which any Russian export controls will be administered. The careers and movements of the 400 or so Russian scientists who were involved with biological weapons are also of interest to the West.

A great concern in terms of nuclear and other weapons proliferation is that former Soviet nuclear and missile scientists might seek employment in the wider world. While there are perhaps 2,000 or so people with fairly extensive knowledge of nuclear weapons design, and 3–5,000 with experience of uranium enrichment or plutonium production,[73] there must be many more with partial expertise which would be useful to a state seeking to develop its own systems and wishing to fill specific technological gaps.[74] The Iraqi nuclear effort has demonstrated how a state can put together a nuclear programme from a range of sources and countries. Individuals could take with them designs, components and even machines if the export control systems of FSU successor states are not strengthened. To date the West has received repeated reassurances that the sense of responsibility of these people will keep them at home,[75] but sustained economic deprivation, for instance in the isolated, specialized and formerly secret defence cities of Russia, could drive individuals overseas. China and North Korea are reliably reported to have tried to recruit missile scientists and a group of ten such experts may have gone to North Korea in August 1992. A further group was prevented from leaving Russia in October 1992.[76] A Russian poll in 1992 found large numbers of workers throughout the defence sector wanted to leave Russia for a better life.[77]

The personnel issue is clearly part of the large set of security problems associated with the effective redirection of much of the huge former Soviet military sector to civilian purposes. These issues are discussed in the next chapter, but proliferation dangers must remain a specific concern of the West: assessing the various possibilities for proliferation, the US analyst Steve Miller noted that 'conceivably... the break-up of the Soviet Union could produce nine or ten nuclear powers'.[78]

3 FSU SECURITY RISKS: POTENTIAL THREATS FROM MILITARY SECTOR RESOURCES

If the successor states of the former Soviet Union are to have what the West perceives to be the prerequisites for a cooperative international outlook and for stable government – that is, if they are to become expanding market economies run by pluralist democracies – they will have to overcome a series of problems presented by the volume and control of resources which in the past were directed to the military sector. A failure to deal with these would probably mean that the military sector would continue to absorb excessive resources, that domestic economic advance would be retarded, and that the foreign policies of the successor states would put excessive reliance on the threat and use of force. In 1992 the Russian policy analyst, Sergei Rogov, suggested a framework of issues relating to the Russian military which is used as a basis for the discussion below.[1]

(a) Civilian supervision

First, armed forces need to be placed under civilian and preferably democratic control, which will mean the installation of civil service staffs (with capability in such areas as defence policy-making and procurement, and military doctrine) and the strengthening of appropriate parliamentary supervision, even direction, of defence policy. The political control over the armed forces enjoyed by the Communist Party and the Defence Council of the former Soviet Union has disappeared,[2] with the Russian Security Council appearing a much less powerful substitute. While the West is offering much advice, there is no established best practice on these matters and many approaches are used by different Western democracies. The Russian Federation Law on Defence specified the Russian president as commander in chief of Russia's armed forces and asserted the Supreme Soviet's right to approve the military budget and military doctrine, but in 1992 it was left to the General Staff to draw up the latter (as noted) and to design force structures. The law left unclear the role of the Supreme Soviet in the choice of defence minister,[3] although the Congress of People's Deputies at least temporarily obtained the right to select the defence and other key ministers at the end of 1992.[4] General Shaposhnikov, as CIS commander, was under no formal political control as there was no CIS political authority to which he had to report.

President Yeltsin's 1993 constitution gave the right to appoint ministers to the president, acting with the consent of the prime minister. The president also appoints the high command of the Russian armed forces. In Yeltsin's Russia, the military were led by 45-year-old Defence Minister General Pavel Grachev, with a high command of an average age of 48, dominated by the Chief of the General Staff and First Deputy Defence Minister, Colonel General Mikhail P. Kolesnikov. Although the 1993 military doctrine paid lip-service to governmental control over the military, soldiers clearly enjoyed *de facto* control of the defence ministry and had successfully resisted pressures for major change.[5]

Significantly, the dimensions of political uncertainty in Russia still include the possibility that democracy may fail to develop, that authoritarian rule could return, and even that military authorities could seize power.

In 1994 Russia's political system remains in a period of transition. The struggle between President Yeltsin and the Congress of People's Deputies, which began in December 1992 and continued until the tragic scenes of October 1993, emphasized that the country was not clear as to whether it would be primarily a parliamentary or a presidential democracy. President Yeltsin did not find it easy in 1992 to keep in close contact with opinion in the Congress of People's

Deputies,[6] whose speaker, Ruslan Khasbulatov, proclaimed after the fall of Mr Gaidar that 'Congress has established itself as the supreme organ of state power'.[7] Formally Russia operated under a modified version of the old (1978) Soviet constitution until the December 1993 elections brought approval for a new constitution. However, President Yeltsin's position, having been considerably strengthened by his partial success in the April 1993 referendum, was weakened by the unexpectedly large vote for the nationalists in the December elections.[8]

By the late spring of 1994, *The Economist* at least felt that there were some grounds for optimism about the increasing stability of the Russian political system,[9] yet in the longer term Russia may not develop into a pluralistic democracy at all. Political parties have only shallow roots and the essence of democracy, which is that politicians accept the loss of elections, has little history in Russia. There was much speculation about a possible seizure of power by the armed forces during 1992 and 1993. At the General Staff level the armed forces appear more autonomous, given the collapse of Party and KGB control. One possibility is that Russia could keep a civilian, even elected, government, but that the military would emerge as largely autonomous, able to win large resources for their activities and to exercise a major influence on foreign policy. President Yeltsin clearly owes something to the military for their backing in October 1993 and the possibility remains that the price could be high over the longer term. In early 1994 the armed forces seemed to have been demanding rewards in terms of higher troop numbers (2.1 million as opposed to a planned 1.5 million), higher defence spending, and continued deployment of Russian troops beyond Russia in some areas of the former Soviet Union, all in return for their earlier support for President Yeltsin. The higher troop numbers and the bases appear to have been accepted by Yeltsin. However, at least in the first half of 1994, the government refused to provide a sufficiently large defence budget to pay for soldiers' salaries and even a minimal amount for equipment. Without funds it is doubtful whether either the troop numbers or the bases in the CIS will be sustainable, but it is also unclear how long the government will resist the pressure to increase the defence budget, or how many resources will flow to the defence sector from sources outside the defence budget.

Despite the claims of the anti-Yeltsin Officers' Union about its own strength,[10] an effective coup is unlikely while the memories of August 1991 and October 1993 are still fresh, and while the armed forces are so occupied with the simple tasks of surviving, maintaining discipline and having somewhere to live.[11] Defence Minister General Grachev had been adamant in early 1993 that the Russian military would not interfere in politics and in October 1992 the defence ministry (as well as the security and interior ministries) reportedly rejected a proposal that the President should suspend the parliament.[12] The military's involvement in politics was thus extremely reluctant in October 1993 and was undertaken only when it was clear that the army would not be required to attack a civilian crowd. Brian Taylor has observed that 'the Russian military has no tradition of intervention in politics, is not running the country and has no desire to take power in the future ... The Russian armed forces would rather do almost anything, including pick potatoes, than try to rule their turbulent country'.[13] Moreover, the conscription system remains in disarray and it could be argued that a coup would be more feasible if Russia had a completely professional army.

In the meantime, Moscow's ability to control units of the Russian army deployed outside Russia remains in some doubt, for instance in the Dnestr region of Moldova.[14] Loss of control and the breakdown of discipline are clearly more likely if the centre continues to be unable to pay its professional soldiers a viable salary on schedule.

In the longer term, a military attempt to seize power cannot be ruled out[15] but apparently it is more likely that forces of conservatism and perhaps nationalism will take over, led perhaps by industrial leaders and former Vice-President Rutskoi, who was not kept in prison despite his anti-Yeltsin efforts in October 1993 and who now chairs the People's Party of Free Russia. A government could rule through the remaining former Soviet bureaucracies and traditional industrial elites.[16] The long-term power of Zhirinovsky's Liberal Democratic ultra-nationalist party also cannot be ignored but in this respect the words of James Sherr may be particularly pertinent. He wrote that 'as the dust settles, we are likely to find that, with the exception of the Communist Party apparatus, power is held by the successors to the KGB, the Armed Forces, the military-industrial complex and the state bureaucracy'. He wrote of the '750,000 people who really run Russia. Half of these people are unreconstructed and probably unreformable. The other half want to change ... but for the most part do not know how. So long as these people think and work in traditional ways, even the most radical Russian President will be nothing more than the titular head of his country'.[17]

Another telling observation is that of Philip Hanson: 'The image of local power in Russia that the observer now receives is one in which the old order survives, with a few exceptions, at the local level, without the network of the Party that formally linked local elites to the centre. The danger is of 78 Albanias.'[18]

Almost all experts agree that it would be impossible to restore communist totalitarianism, since the lies and myths of the former regime have been fully exposed. But an authoritarian system, presumably seeing itself as 'socialist' and appealing strongly to Russian nationalist sentiments, would surely soon need to use extensive repression in such a diverse country.[19] Sherr wrote of Russia that, 'if those who hold legal power continue to make concessions to those who hold real power, we might end up with failure and instability'.[20]

While the central political authorities in Russia are so unpredictable in their character, and a significant element of the Russian population is being drawn to crude nationalist slogans, there are grounds for arguing that effective civilian control over the Russian military should not be a pressing Western priority. However, in the longer term, an autonomous Russian military (which would clearly produce an enormous demand for resources) is something that both the West and Russians themselves would have to see as problematic.

In Ukraine and the CIS republics the military dominate defence policy-making.[21] Even in states (including Ukraine and the Baltic states) where civilian defence ministers are in place, the amount of civilian expertise on defence matters is clearly limited. Thus the effective democratic and civilian supervision of defence will take a long time to establish, requiring as it does political authorities with the ambition for control, a cooperative military, and civilians in defence ministries and parliaments who have security and defence expertise.

(b) Forces restructuring

Next, the former Soviet army has to be reorganized and the Russian army and other republics need to establish their own forces. Leaving aside conscripts, the 1992 Russian army included some 1.4 million officers and career non-commissioned officers, not all of whom were Russian. Russia plans a multi-stage development of its armed forces to end by the start of the next century. The armed forces, which will have been cut to 2.1 million by 1995, were supposed to fall further to an apparently arbitrary figure, resented by some officers,[22] of 1.5 million, which would be one per cent of the Russian population. As noted Defence Minister Grachev apparently got the target raised to 2.1 million after the October 1993 crisis although even by February 1994 the army seems to have downgraded its establishment target to under two million.[23]

However, a concern with numbers diverts attention from the extensive disruption in the Russian army caused by shortages of funds and troops. In 1994 the conscription system is near complete break-down with many of those being called up not reporting for duty, and there have been many officers' complaints about the health and other qualities of conscripts. The army has also had little success in recruiting the number of contract troops it had hoped for[24] and those signed up are proving considerably more expensive than expected.[25] As a consequence, many units are drastically undermanned and further reorganization of the armed forces must be expected.

In principle, Ukrainians could have gone into the Ukrainian armed forces, Belarussians into the Belarussian forces and so on, with some leeway for those who wished to continue to serve a different republic from their own. Many 'foreign' officers seem to have been reluctant to leave their units because of accommodation problems in their home state. In the autumn of 1992, some 320,000 Ukrainians were serving in foreign forces,[26] and in the spring of 1994 some 20 per cent of the Russian army officer corps was non-Russian.[27] Yet keeping individuals in place presented problems, as the divisions and stresses caused by the Ukrainian government's efforts to have sailors in the Black Sea Fleet take an oath of allegiance to Ukraine revealed. The break-up of the Soviet Union left Ukraine with some of the elite units of the Soviet armed forces, although 25 per cent of army officers subsequently refused to take an oath of allegiance to Ukraine.[28] As the make-up of Ukrainian and Russian peace-keeping forces in former Yugoslavia indicates, their forces are still not homogeneous and many professional military in the former Soviet Union seem drawn to almost any national force which offers them decent pay and conditions.

Ukraine produced a four-stage military plan in which the first stage, in 1992–3, involved the establishment of forces and mechanisms of command. In 1993–4 a plan for the strategic use of the armed forces was developed (see section (f) below), and in 1995 a system for mobile deployment is to be established. By then, force numbers will have been reduced from the original level of 650,000 to around 400,000, thus easing current accommodation shortages. In the fourth stage, by the year 2000, Ukraine's forces will be cut to their target level of 220,000.[29] Politically there was a debate in Ukraine as to how far the main threat should be acknowledged as coming from Russia, and while the nationalist Ukrainian Republican Party advocated much larger forces (of around 500,000), the Ukrainian government also recognized that further cuts were possible.[30] Problems in running defence on a day-to-day basis in Ukraine led to a failure to pay troops, civil-military disputes over appointments and the resignation of seven senior generals in early 1994.[31] Ukraine was the only post-Soviet republic to challenge Russia's inheritance of all the former Soviet navy, and the dispute over the Black Sea Fleet persisted for more than the first two years of the modern

Ukraine's life. By the summer of 1994 Ukraine had conceded that Russia could inherit the great bulk of the fleet (80 per cent) in return for Russian compensation for about a quarter of the ships. Yet difficulties persisted in negotiations on where Russia could base the fleet. Russia fundamentally sought to keep the ships in their existing plurality of bases, in part because shore accommodation for naval personnel was available, whereas Ukraine wanted the fleet concentrated in one place (Donuzlav).[32] This dispute may eventually be settled by a financial arrangement in which Russia would pay for what it uses, but it may alternatively drag on, leading to a further deterioration in Russian-Ukrainian relations. Any Russian rent paid for bases in the Black Sea would imply that the Russian government had given up hope of seeing Crimea returned to Russia, and would raise issues in Ukraine about who would benefit from the received rents.

In other republics, the establishment of national armed forces is proceeding with difficulty, not least because of a shortage of military expertise and money. Belarus has complained about the number of its air force personnel who have left to serve in Russia, presumably for economic reasons,[33] and the Belarus-born proportion of its armed forces, while rising sharply, will not reach 65 per cent before 1995.[34] Georgia, understandably in view of its internal conflicts, faced daunting problems in seeking to organize armed forces. In the Soviet armed forces, 75 per cent of officers had been Russian and 90 per cent Slav (i.e. Russian, Belarussian and Ukrainian).[35]

A framework for the reorganization of several former Soviet forces is the CFE Treaty of 1990 and the related agreement on manpower ceilings, both of which were signed by the Soviet Union. The force entitlements agreed have since had to be divided among several relevant Soviet successor states. While allocating forces and assets simply on the basis of their distribution prior to the break-up of the Soviet Union was seen by Russia as giving it an unfairly small allocation,[36] an agreement was concluded in the summer of 1992 (see Table 3). Its implementation, which will take time and therefore may be disrupted by political developments, gives very large entitlements of

Table 3: Maximum level of treaty limited equipment holdings in the former Soviet Union and Eastern Europe and maximum personnel levels

Area	Tanks	ACVs	Artillery	Aircraft	Helicopters	Personnel
Armenia	220	220	285	100	50	no declars.
Azerbaijan	220	220	285	100	50	no declars.
Belarus	1,800	2,600	1,615	260	80	100,000
Georgia	220	220	285	100	50	no declars.
Moldova	210	210	250	50	50	no declars.
Russia	6,400	11,890	6,415	3,450	890	1,450,000
Ukraine	4,080	5,050	4,040	1,090	330	450,000
Total CIS	13,150	20,000	13,175	5,150	1,500	n.a.
Bulgaria	1,475	2,000	1,750	235	67	104,000
Czechoslovakia	1,435	2,050	1,150	345	75	140,000
Hungary	835	1,700	840	180	108	n.a.
Poland	1,730	2,150	1,610	460	130	234,000
Romania	1,375	2,100	1,475	430	120	230,248
Total East Europe	6,850	10,000	6,825	1,650	500	n.a.

Source: Lynn E. Davis (Project Director), *An Arms Control Strategy for the New Europe*, Santa Monica, Rand Corp., 1993, pp. 12–13.

air and land equipment to Ukraine, among others. Armenia and Azerbaijan took quick advantage of the equipment which they acquired from former Soviet forces to step up hostilities in their war over Nagorny Karabakh. Some difficulties were caused by the allocation of combat and transport aircraft in the FSU, including the Asian republics beyond the CFE area.[37]

In the spring of 1994, Russia began to complain once more about the allocations in the CFE Treaty and in particular about the restricted deployments it was allowed to make on its periphery, especially in the Caucasus, which it perceived as a new area of instability. In particular, Russia would like to be able to deploy more armour in the Caucasus region than the CFE Treaty allows and indeed may be doing so. In exchange, it may be happy to deploy fewer forces in the Kaliningrad area, which should reduce Russian–Lithuanian friction. Despite Russian dissatisfaction with one element in the CFE Treaty, it remains valuable as a basis from which several CIS states can work to structure their armed forces. It provides some kind of conceptual framework in a disintegrating state where otherwise no guidance would have been available.

(c) Force redeployment and accommodation

Forces have to be redeployed and accommodated. By early 1994 Russia was well advanced in the process of bringing home some 800,000 troops and their equipment from Germany and Eastern Europe.[38] In Soviet times up to 200,000 troops had been stationed in the three Baltic states. By early 1992 the new Baltic governments were demanding the withdrawal of all these forces as soon as possible. This proved to be much more problematic than the moves out of Central Europe. In the spring of 1992, because of accommodation problems but perhaps also because of political reluctance, Russian forces remained in the Baltic states, to the consternation and resentment of the small states' governments.[39] However, by the winter of 1992, the withdrawal was once more proceeding steadily, although during the autumn President

Yeltsin had announced a halt in Estonia and Latvia, alleging discrimination by their governments against their Russian inhabitants.[40] Another hold-up was announced by General Grachev in March 1993, apparently because of Estonia and Latvia's refusal to pay for the withdrawal and relocation costs.[41] Since the troop withdrawal from the Baltics has been marked more by friction in Russian-Baltic state relations than by difficulties in Russian military organizations, it is discussed more fully in Chapter 4.

As part of its deal with the FSU on unification, Germany is paying for the building of many dwellings in Russia for officers formerly based in Germany but this expenditure alone cannot resolve the accommodation shortage. The organizational achievements of the Russian army in moving so many troops and equipment in such a brief period are considerable, as those involved with the much more modest reduction of UK forces in Germany could testify. However, in 1994 many Russian forces are still deployed throughout the FSU without any legal basis having been agreed for their presence, or any timetable arranged for their withdrawal. This is a matter of some concern to the Congress of People's Deputies.[42] Russia is therefore looking to conclude bilateral agreements in the political context of the CIS to provide for Russian bases in a range of non-Russian republics including Georgia but excluding Ukraine.

Overall it will be important to establish force structures throughout the CIS which do not alarm neighbours, and here the CFE1(a) agreement on manpower ceilings could play a valuable role. However, Russia's main aim by 1994 was to coordinate and dominate many armed forces in the FSU by building up the CIS, with its own command, as a collective security body. It had apparently given up hope, however, of creating CIS forces as such.

(d) Military budgets

Again throughout the FSU, military budgets have had to be cut and reshaped. Under the former Soviet Union approximately 17 per cent of Soviet GNP was devoted to defence[43] and some 50 per cent of military expenditure went on equipment. The latter is being cut drastically (Russian equipment spending was reduced by about 68 per cent in 1992,[44] increased slightly in 1993[45] but appears to have been dramatically reduced again in 1994). Procurement proposals from the finance ministry were said to have been pared down in 1994 to 45 per cent of their 1993 level in roubles (10 per cent in dollar terms). The finance ministry seemingly proposed 5.5 trillion roubles ($3 billion) for procurement whereas the defence ministry wanted 28.3 trillion roubles ($18 million).[46] The priority for Russian forces in 1994 is likely to be finding the money to pay the professional officers and NCOs.[47] Yet, given the long-term aspirations of senior Russian officers to deploy extremely sophisticated equipment, especially in the areas of command, control, communication and intelligence, and of advanced conventional munitions, persistent friction can be expected between the government and the military; in 1994 both the Russian armed forces and the defence industry were complaining vigorously about the inadequate resources allocated to them in the draft budget,[48] and in the middle of the year the level of planned spending reportedly set by the Duma (40,600 billion roubles) was 14,400 billion roubles less than the military said was the absolute minimum needed.[49]

(e) Professionalism

The professionalization of the Russian forces, needed for reasons of demography, technology and economics, will present challenges of organization and philosophy. Russia will not need many more professional troops given its envisaged armed forces of about 1.5 million, but it will need to release some and attract others. It is planned that, by 1995, '35 per cent of all servicemen will have been recruited on a contract basis and by the year 2000 50 per cent of all privates and sergeants will have been recruited by contract'.[50] None of this will be easy given the deteriorating reputation of the armed forces in Russia (which could in principle be halted by professionalization) and the growing reluctance of draftees to serve[51] (as Moscow Radio put it on 12 February 1994, 'if there are no soldiers there is no army'). However, because of the unexpectedly high costs of contract troops according to Russian figures, it is also doubtful whether Russia will be able to afford as many as the army would like.

(f) Strategies and doctrines

The armed forces of the new republics and other East European states need strategies and doctrines to guide their operation and development. Preferably these should be compatible with the goals of the CSCE process and CFE Treaty so that security relations within Eastern Europe as a whole are marked by mutual reassurance rather than by mutual provocation and alarm, leading to arms competition and conflicts. There is cause for concern. As noted earlier, Russia's military doctrine asserts the protection of Russians outside Russia as one of the identified missions of its armed forces. The initial draft military doctrine of Ukraine was rejected by parliament in the autumn of 1992 and in April 1993 because of its neglect of the nuclear dimension. It finally became law in October 1993 and included the provision that Ukraine 'will regard as a potential enemy all states that have territorial claims against Ukraine, interfere in its internal affairs, form or join alliances directed against the political, economic and military interests of Ukraine'.[52] Since significant elements in Russia believe their country has a legitimate claim on the Crimea, it must be concluded that Ukraine will prepare explicitly against a Russian threat (although the doctrine refers to a need to repulse aggression from all directions). The doctrine stated that Ukrainian armed forces could not be used to deal with internal political problems, that servicemen could not take part in political activities and that Ukraine rejected unilateral disarmament. On the nuclear issue, it asserted that the use of nuclear weapons was unacceptable, and that while 'circumstances have made Ukraine a nuclear power ... the country will never threaten, never mind use, nuclear weapons. It intends to become a non-nuclear power in the future'.[53] The doctrine was somewhat ambiguous, even contradictory, on some issues. For instance, it spoke of maintaining a universal obligation to serve, yet referred to the aim of a long-term move to a professional army. Also Ukraine was to maintain its non-bloc status yet the doctrine supported the development of regional security systems and collective action. As in Russian thinking, there was an emphasis on the value of high-technology weapons and the doctrine indicated that Ukraine would try to maintain its defence industrial base, preferably in forms which supported civil industrial production. However, procurement was presented as clearly secondary to soldiers' pay and conditions. While much of the document, which was particularly concerned with large-scale conventional war, was inspired by the perceived danger from Russia,[54] it would appear to provide only a rough guide for the future development of Ukrainian forces.

Around the former Soviet Union, successor states are seeking to develop foreign and security policy thinking on the basic characteristics of their position and how they are to react in terms of military preparations. When so many governments have so little military experience, and when the political environment is so uncertain, developing such thinking in ways which provide a basis for defence policy but which do not alarm neighbours is rarely straightforward. Turkmenistan's military doctrine, for example, which was announced in March 1994, said that the country would be guided by a policy of self-defence, positive neutrality, and non-interference in the affairs of others. There would be no foreign forces on its territory and it would form no blocs. However, the doctrine also indicated that the country would rely for armaments and much other help on Russia, and that Russian servicemen would continue to be welcome to serve in Turkmenistan's armed forces.[55]

(g) The defence industry

Finally, in terms of the adjustment of defence and the military, the defence industry and technology need to be converted and controlled.

For their own economic benefit, the successor republics need to reduce their defence effort drastically, preferably to five per cent or less of national output, in line with Western efforts. Moreover, they need to accompany such a change by utilizing effectively in the civil area the resources previously devoted to the military sector. This is a formidable task especially for Russia and Ukraine. These defence resources include the human and capital assets organized previously for defence production and the soldiers no longer needed for the armed forces.

The difficulties associated with converting the economy (indeed the society) of the FSU from a military to a civil character are legion. No matter how daunting the task, the need to retrain officers so that they can usefully serve the civil sector will have to be addressed. Some 600,000 officers and NCOs may have been made redundant from the Red Army during 1992. Although some progress was made,[56] industrial conversion efforts in the early 1990s in the FSU were not marked by frequent success.[57] Individual plants and firms faced different combinations of problems associated with conversion, which makes generalization difficult.[58] But Russia and Ukraine could not and cannot afford to write off all the capital associated with their 2,000-plus defence-oriented research and manufacturing enterprises, however hard it is to change non-market-oriented, highly inefficient factories into viable units.[59] Statistics underline the fact that the sector was over-manned: at the time of separation, Russian defence-industrial facilities employed about 6.5 million people and those of Ukraine about 1.2 million.[60] This was about 4.4 per cent and 2.9 per cent respectively of the population of the two countries. In contrast, Britain's defence industry, which was often considered to be disproportionately large, only employed about 1.1 per cent of the population even at the height of the Cold War. In addition to manufacturing facilities, Soviet defence firms frequently operated extensive and expensive social and support facilities which could not easily be absorbed by firms producing for a competitive market. For instance, the Saratov Aviation Plant (which makes the Yak 42) in 1993 employed 14,000 workers directly and another 5,000 on neighbouring farms which produced the food for its workforce.[61] The official Russian approach is to support with subsidies only those factories which produce equipment needed for the Russian armed forces, and those which convert to civilian production yielding substitutes for imported goods. About 250 billion roubles ($454 million) was supposedly allocated by Russia to promote defence conversion in 1993 and 700 billion roubles in 1994. Factories are not supposed to be subsidized to export arms.[62] However, to accept the social costs associated with the rigorous application of such guidelines has so far been very difficult for any Russian government.

Neither Russia nor Ukraine could or should contemplate the complete disappearance of their defence industries, although one UN-based study which concluded that conversion was mainly a matter for the Russian nuclear industry rather than its conventional arms sector surely overstated the position.[63] Russia and Ukraine will clearly try to continue to maintain significant armed forces and will want to supply them from their own industries, but that should require much less industrial capacity than was inherited from the former Soviet days.

Failure to address the conversion issue across the board would mean that Russian and Ukrainian enterprises might be drawn further towards irresponsible sales of conventional and even non-conventional defence technology (a temptation to which Western firms may not be immune). In times of persistent economic dislocation, governments will be tempted to endorse arms export deals which under other circumstances they would reject. By February 1994 the Russian defence-industrial sector appeared to be resisting further demands for conversion in the face of a declining civil economy and simply grinding to a halt through an absence of state orders and the refusal of the state to pay alleged debts of 1,500 billion roubles to defence enterprises. Production between 1991 and 1994 fell by as much as 78 per cent.[64] According to a report on Moscow radio, in February 1994 nearly 70 per cent of the plants for supplying the Russian defence ministry were 'standing idle'.[65]

As former Soviet defence firms are pressed towards imprudent and perhaps illegal defence exports in order to survive, and to earn the hard foreign exchange that is so valuable in countries where there is no reliable domestic currency, the practical export control problems facing their government need to be highlighted. Under the strict former Soviet regime, the scope for evading state controls was small but these controls disappeared with the collapse of the Soviet Union and they have not been properly replaced. The signs are that nuclear technology probably remains under control for the moment, although there are persistent reports of sensitive materials being available for sale.[66] Certainly light arms and even heavier equipment can be smuggled from Russia and other republics, despite the establishment of 64 new customs posts on Russia's borders.[67] Unauthorized arms sales were thought to be occurring by 1992, although the government insisted it had full control, and rumours of arms smuggling, often involving Kaliningrad and the Baltic states, have continued to appear.[68] Despite the Russian government's approval in May 1992 of guidelines to restrict the transfer of dual-use technology, its intention to join the Missile Technology Control regime, its participation in the UN Security Council Permanent Five talks on the conventional arms trade,[69] and Yeltsin's approval of a list of goods requiring export licences,[70] it can be expected that, under conditions of sustained economic deprivation, the Russian government (and others, including that of Ukraine) will be less inclined to exercise restrictive controls, and that companies and others will be more desperate to evade those that are in place.

The appropriate administration of conventional arms export controls is a problematic matter even in the West, where the balance of responsibility for promoting sales and providing finance between companies and government varies from state to state. In all arms-exporting countries there are tensions between the government's duty to restrain and control arms exports, and its role in furthering them. In contemporary Russia the situation is particularly fluid, as factories and firms explore the need and opportunity for more autonomy and different sections of the government compete for influence.

The export control system was formally focused on the General Department for Military and Technical Cooperation of the Ministry of

Foreign Economic Relations. The Oberonexport organization (formerly under Vice Prime Minister Georgi Khiza) claimed a major role in marketing and licensing for specialized military equipment[71] but individual factories and firms were thought to be unhappy with its efforts. A further body was the General Department for Cooperation at the Ministry for Foreign Economic Relations (GUSK) which also claimed to be able to sell defence equipment from factories and from stockpiles, and which had the task of promoting technological cooperation. In aerospace, Aviaexport marketed military as well as civil aircraft, including Antonov aircraft from Ukraine. Formally the Ministry for Foreign Economic Relations was responsible for administering end-user certificates.

As Russian arms marketing became increasingly confused, the system for the promotion and control of exports was amended further in 1993 and 1994 with the Rosvooruzheniye state company being placed in formal control over Oberonexport, GUSK and Spetzvneshtekhnika (which arranged technical assistance). There was industrial concern, however, that the new company was responsible to the defence ministry rather than industry, indeed its president was named as former Soviet Defence Minister and CIS Commander in Chief, Yevgeny Shaposhnikov.[72] His possible lack of sympathy for defence enterprises was signalled in his observation that 'Russia will observe UN embargoes. The state's reputation should not be blemished for the sake of a million or even several hundred million dollars'.[73] In 1994, therefore, Russia looked keen to export arms, but not in an uncontrolled or irresponsible way. However, Western doubts were reasonable, both with regard to Russia's ability to prevent smuggling, especially of light arms, and its long-term capability to resist industrial pressure for licences to almost any cash customer. Rosvooruzheniye's domination was in doubt even by June 1994 as companies sought greater freedom to market their wares.[74]

There are also some specialized military resources which need to be dismantled and placed in safe storage. In particular, without outside help Russia will not dispose in a form acceptable to the West of the 150 nuclear attack and 30 nuclear missile submarines which it no longer requires.[75] Russia has previously dumped unwanted submarine reactors in both its western and eastern oceans, and in 1994 there are 23 obsolete submarines in the Arctic awaiting destruction. Most have their fuel rods still in their reactors.[76]

Unless these difficulties related to the defence sector are reasonably managed across the FSU, that sector will prove a continuing problem for successor states' economies and for their political systems, as well as for proliferation efforts and the promotion of cooperative international relations. The redirection of defence resources remains an immense and multi-dimensional task: as Christopher Donnelly has written, 'the Soviet Union ... did not have a war machine, it was a war machine'.[77]

Clearly the defence-industrial sector and its re-orientation towards civil production, and issues of future political system stability, cannot be considered in isolation from wider economic matters. Significantly, as late as 1994 the longer-term shape of the Russian, Ukrainian and many other successor state economies had not yet been determined.

Economic collapse in the first half of 1992 was worse in the Transcaucasus and the Asian republics than in Russia, and Belarus and Ukraine did not fare significantly better.[78] There was further deterioration in 1993, yet Moscow often sees itself in a better position than other nearby states and views itself as 'the stronghold of stability among its newly independent neighbours'. Although the accuracy of the statistics must clearly be doubted, not least because of the size of the unrecorded black economy, especially in Russia, CIS figures issued in February 1994 illustrated the gravity of the situation. They showed that in the five richest CIS states (Russia, Belarus, Ukraine, Kazakhstan and Moldova), national income was down by 32 per cent or more in 1993 compared with 1991. The situation in other republics was in many ways worse.[79] With such economic dislocation over a sustained period, people will become ever more despondent and/or desperate, so imperilling any political system.

In the spring of 1994 it is hard to see just what sort of economic system could eventually emerge in Russia. *The Economist* has seen real grounds for optimism, noting that reform was possible and citing a nineteenth-century view of Japan that 'Wealthy we do not think it could ever be. The love of indolence and pleasure of the people forbid it.'[80] In principle, if the Japanese could change, so could the Russians. Although by July 1993 the position looked better than it had done for some time, with inflation down to 15 per cent a month and the rouble regaining a little value against the dollar, the rouble had not been truly stabilized. The major state monopolies remained in place and in need of huge subsidies. A further burst of government spending fuelled further inflation. Surprisingly, in the spring of 1994 Prime Minister Chernomyrdin placed restraints on spending (and inflation), but there were real doubts about how long he could resist demands from the defence sector and elsewhere for more state money. The Russian economy may be marked by regular major bursts of inflation caused by increased government spending. In the Russian economy overall, the legal system did not provide reliable encouragement for foreign or domestic investment. Capitalists were often associated with the criminal sector and the activities of organized crime were a growing deterrent to national and foreign investment. Taxes were so high that tax avoidance was massive, indeed necessary for many enterprises. There had been extensive privatization but major enterprises still looked to the state for subsidies. Russians, fearing political turmoil, were reluctant to invest in their firms. Russia asserted a wish to move to a market economy but had little notion of how markets needed to be regulated.[81]

Ukraine and many other successor states had also made minimal progress towards economic reform and had significantly failed to establish stable national currencies. The Baltic states were fortunately an exception in this respect.

In summary, the security significance both of the problems of redirecting defence resources into the civilian sector and of the difficulties which FSU states face in trying to introduce economic reform and growth in general is apparent. The links between economic progress, political stability and cooperative international relationships are widely asserted in the West. Certainly, if economic decline in the FSU cannot be arrested, it is hard to see how democracy can develop and authoritarian nationalist forces be kept at bay. In Russia and Ukraine especially, with their Soviet heritage of large armed forces and defence industry, unless defence resources can be effectively channelled into the civil sector, general economic progress – already difficult – will be greatly hindered. Moreover, it will be hard for Russia and other successor states of the Soviet Union to introduce efficient use of defence resources and effective supervision, and to develop defence doctrines and postures which do not promote national security by generating fear and concern in others.

4 FSU SECURITY RISKS: POLITICAL PROBLEMS AND MILITARY SOLUTIONS?

The FSU is beset with many political problems which either already involve violence or could lead to violence in the near future.[1] Many of these stem from the contrast between the often-asserted abstract right of national self-determination through statehood and the reality that Europe does not divide up easily into specified areas, each inhabited by the people of one 'nation'. Not surprisingly, proposals to change boundaries usually generate major resistance.

The break-up of the Soviet Union at the end of 1991 was based on the understanding that the internal borders of the constituent Soviet republics would become the external borders of the new sovereign states, or at least that force would not be used to change those borders. It is uncertain how long this understanding will be sustained, especially as there were many disputed areas even when the Soviet Union was in being. The Institute of Geography of the Soviet Academy of Sciences calculated in 1991 that, of the 23 borders linking CIS states, only three were not contested.[2]

The FSU is facing a multitude of minority problems and disputes. These fall into three main categories:[3]

(1) where people from the ethnic/national group of one state live in part in another state (for example, the Russians who live in Kazakhstan, the 'Romanians' who live in Moldova, the Poles who live in Ukraine and Belarus, and the 900,000 Tajiks in Uzbekistan). Some of these minority problems clearly cross the external borders of the former Soviet Union;

(2) where a national/ethnic group without a state lives within one state (for example, the 100,000 Abkhazians in Georgia and the Tatars in Russia);
(3) where a national/ethnic group without a state lives in more than one state (for example the Ossetians of Georgia and Russia).

The daunting nature of these problems was effectively summarized by Stephen Van Evera:

> The former USSR's population totals some 262 million people, comprising 104 nationalities. Of these a total of 64 million (24 per cent) either live outside their home republic, or are among the 89 small nationalities with no titular republic, and who are thus minorities in the Soviet Union's 15 successor states ... Of these 64 million, some 39 million ... are members of nationalities that have a titular republic, but live outside it; these include 24 million Russians (17 per cent of all Russians) and 15 million members of other nationalities (15 per cent of all such nationalities). Another 25 million people (9 per cent of the total Soviet population) are members of the 89 smaller nationalities without titular home republics, who will be minorities wherever they live.[4]

Central to the ethnic and national problems which cross the state frontiers of the successor states are those of Russia and the Russians. Here there is increased uncertainty because of both the strengths and the weaknesses of Russian nationalism.

Hélène Carrère d'Encausse has written of the break-up of the Soviet Union as 'the triumph of the nations'[5] and, if the principle of national self-determination is promoted with vigour by Russia, there could be a much larger Russia than that in place in 1994. Strong nationalist sentiment is associated in Russia not only with neo-fascist elements such as the Liberal Democratic Party[6] but also with 'centrists' such as former Vice-President Rutskoi. There are between 20 and 25 million people considering themselves as Russians who live in other parts of the former Soviet Union, some having moved from their homeland essentially as colonialists. Extending the Russian state to include them would at least involve Russia's absorbing Crimea from Ukraine, large chunks of Kazakhstan, and parts of Estonia and Latvia where Russians are in a majority.[7] On the other hand, tens of thousands of Russians are continuing to return to Russia each year[8] and, should more and more of these 25 million be driven back by hostile political and economic pressures in their existing homes, political relations between Russia and the former Soviet republics concerned would be damaged. In addition the Russian economy would have to generate even more housing and jobs.[9] Some Russians assert that a role of the CIS is to be a source of reassurance for many Russians living outside the Russian Federation.[10] Table 4 shows the percentage of Russians in the successor states of the FSU.

But a quite different trend towards a smaller Russia is also possible. Conflict may arise from secessionist movements within Russia itself, where there is no clear idea of which groups can reasonably claim the status of 'nation' entitled to form a sovereign state. The Russian Federation includes 20 autonomous republics and different groups have different views on the degree of autonomy from Moscow to which they should be entitled.[11] By the middle of 1992 the people of Chechen Ingushetia were struggling to form two republics in that autonomous but ethnically varied region and by 1993 Chechnya considered itself separate from Russia. There was a nationalist movement for Tatarstan to become an independent member of the CIS, its oil-rich neighbour Bashkortostan having won considerable freedom of action. Though very different cases, neither the Muslim Chechnya nor Tatarstan would sign the Russian Federal Treaty of March 1992 which, in part through ambiguous wording, had sought to settle the issue.[12] Sakha, formerly Yakutia, a huge, sparsely populated area which produces 98 per cent of Russia's diamonds, declared itself sovereign.[13] The whole Vladivostok area could move towards independence in the longer term if its psychological distance from Moscow is stretched by growing economic ties with Asian-Pacific states and should its fear of China diminish.

Table 4: Percentage of Russians in the successor states of the former Soviet Union

Successor state	1979	1989	Percentage of other non-locals in 1989	Total 1989 population (millions)
Russia	82.6	81.4	18.6	147.4
Ukraine	21.1	21.9	5.8	51.7
Belarus	11.9	13.1	9.4	10.2
Moldova	12.8	12.9	22.7	4.3
Lithuania	8.9	9.3	11.4	3.7
Latvia	32.8	33.8	14.4	2.7
Estonia	27.9	30.3	8.6	1.6
Georgia	7.4	6.2	24.3	5.5
Azerbaijan	7.9	5.6	11.8	7.0
Armenia	2.3	1.6	4.5	3.3
Kazakhstan	40.8	30.7	22.8	16.5
Kyrgyzstan	25.9	21.4	16.8	4.3
Uzbekistan	10.8	8.3	10.7	19.9
Tajikistan	10.4	7.6	30.4	5.1
Turkmenistan	12.6	9.5	18.8	3.5

Sources: Hélène Carrère d'Encausse, *The End of the Soviet Empire: The Triumph of the Nations*, New York, Basic Books, 1993, p. 222; J.C. Oliphant, *Nationalities Problems in the Former Soviet Union*, Sandhurst, RMA, June 1992.

Russia, it must not be forgotten, stretches across 11 time zones. Stenseth compared the Russian Federation with an onion: 'once you start to peel it, there might be nothing left in the end'.[14]

Daniel Patrick Moynihan's sweeping analysis of the impact of the asserted right of national self-determination and the durability and intensity of ethnic feeling certainly suggests that Russia will break up, and in a disorderly manner. The same forces which ate away at the USSR are at work in Russia itself, and it seems unlikely that the features which Moynihan feels enable multi-ethnic societies to survive – a readiness to live and let live, a sense of humour, and a lack of appreciation of the right of national self-determination – will easily achieve pre-eminence across poverty-stricken Russia.[15] Some analysts believed that, despite the 1992 Federation Treaty, the Russian Federation in 1992 was as near break-up as the USSR had been in 1989. Others, however, felt that a *modus vivendi* was reached during 1992, whereby the centre's rights would be accepted in limited defined areas by regions, which would largely run their own affairs.[16] One model has Russia almost operating on a comparable basis to the Ottoman empire in the nineteenth century, with many areas completely self-ruling. Such a system may well have been brought nearer by President Yeltsin in the spring of 1993 when he sought to use provincial leaders in a Constitutional Assembly against the Congress of People's Deputies in order to secure constitutional change. By offering more powers to the 20 autonomous republics in exchange for their support, Yeltsin provoked some administrative districts of Russia which were territorially and economically significant to demand greater freedom, especially in trade and fiscal affairs. Sverdlesh led the way at the beginning of July 1993 by declaring itself the Urals Republic.[17] While President Yeltsin apparently sought to clamp down on regional autonomy after the failure of the parliament's October 1993 rebellion, ambiguity and uncertainty prevailed.[18] The Treaty of Public Accord of April 1994 seemed unlikely in itself to settle any future structure.[19] While Moscow might peacefully accept the complete loss of some areas, it is more doubtful whether it would peacefully tolerate the secession of territories if the effect would be to take away its own great-power status; yet there must also be doubts that Moscow could control the break-up of Russia once it began. Jessica Stern, pointing to separatism particularly in Tatarstan and the Volga-Ural region, argued that 'the Russian Federation has never been a real state and is not sustainable as a state. Four indicators of centrifugal forces support this claim: lack of agreement about the legitimacy of Russia's current borders; competing economic objectives among different regions of the Federation; competing claims for legitimacy on the part of federal and regional leaders; and the unpredictable allegiance of army units'.[20]

Russo–Ukrainian relations

From the point of view of the international tension, even violence, which could be provoked should relations deteriorate, the Ukrainian-Russian relationship, involving actual or potential disputes about Crimea, eastern Ukraine, the division of the Black Sea Fleet, the ownership and control of the Sevastopol naval base and the control of nuclear weapons, is perhaps the most serious 'international' issue in the FSU.[21] In the middle of 1992 it was apparent that both sides were working to keep the relationship from deteriorating uncontrollably, and many Russian and Ukrainian military officers viewed conflict between them as unthinkable, but forecasts of eventual war between the two states retained some credibility. In July 1993 Russia's parliament overwhelmingly passed a resolution rejecting the June 1993 Moscow agreement by Yeltsin and Kravchuk on the division of the Black Sea Fleet, claiming all the fleet and the port of Sevastopol. The Ukrainian parliamentary reaction, as well as that of Yeltsin, was angry. The so-called Massandra agreement between Yeltsin and Kravchuk in the early autumn of 1993, in which Ukraine was to hand over its share of the Black Sea Fleet to Russia in payment of debts, also proved unacceptable to the Ukrainian parliament. Moreover, in talks on a bilateral defence agreement between the two states, Russia continued to press for special rights in Ukraine and for constraints on Ukraine's freedom of action in security policy, just as it had earlier with other states formerly under its control such as Poland.[22] Russian-Ukrainian relations in early 1993 were marked also by a dispute on energy prices, in which both states sought to maximize their bargaining power. Russia seemed to be seeking political cooperation, even subordination, from Ukraine in exchange for the supply of oil and gas at less than world prices, whereas Ukraine wanted to maximize its revenue from the transit of Russian gas to Western Europe. Claims that Russia was charging lower prices to cooperative states such as Belarus than to difficult states such as Georgia and Ukraine further damaged political relations.

By 1994, the deteriorating and unreformed Ukrainian economy was contributing to the rise of a Russian separatist movement in Crimea and to discontent among the Russians of eastern Ukraine.[23] However, there were signs in the April 1994 parliamentary elections in Ukraine that more Ukrainians, especially in agricultural areas, favoured cooperation with Moscow. The strongest possibilities seemed to be not that Russia might invade, but that Russian areas of Ukraine would seek to secede because of the better economic prospects in Russia, and that more and more Ukrainians would press for a cooperative, i.e. subservient, relationship with Moscow in exchange for anticipated economic benefits.

Ukraine's fears about Moscow's reluctance to accept either its territorial integrity or even its existence as a state have some valid grounds: many Russians find it hard to think of Ukrainians as foreigners and identify more easily with Ukrainians than with 'Russians' in parts of Siberia and the Russian Far East. Russia also refused to sign a treaty of friendship with Ukraine recognizing borders and the rights of minorities[24] though, as noted above, in January 1994 Russian provision was made for extensive security assurances for Ukraine. Although the leaders of Ukraine were eventually able also to agree on a division of the Black Sea Fleet, with Ukraine taking only around 20 per cent of the vessels, arguments about basing arrangements continued through the spring of 1994. The consequences of continued tension in Russo-Ukrainian relations would be far-reaching, not least because Ukraine could revive its efforts to become a nuclear power by developing its own warheads and delivery system. Certainly Russian efforts to intimidate Ukraine alarm Warsaw and lead it to increase its pressure to be allowed to join NATO. In brief, Russo-Ukrainian rivalry could be the basis for a pattern of power politics emerging in the FSU which would spread to East/Central Europe and hinder the wider development of cooperative security. On the other hand, at least in the first half of 1994, Moscow was not encouraging Crimea's elected President, Yuri Meshkow, to press ahead with secession; indeed the Crimean leadership accepted its territory as part of Ukraine.[25] Like other post-Soviet relationships, that between Ukraine and Moscow remains inherently unpredictable.

Russo-Kazakh relations

Similar reasoning could be applied to Russo-Kazakh relations, where a more nationalist government in Moscow might lay claim to the extensive areas of western Kazakhstan where many Russians live. In 1994 the Kazakh government under President Nazarbayev is working for a cooperative relationship with Moscow within the framework of the CIS and claims to want to minimize the impact of ethnic factors in the country's life. Kazakhstan's deteriorating economic position is pushing it towards improved relations with Russia and in the spring of 1994, after difficult negotiations, the two states succeeded in reaching an agreement on Russia's future use of the space launch facilities at the Baykonur cosmodrome. Russia will pay Kazakhstan $115 million a year for the initial 20-year period of the agreement.[26] It was apparent in the 1994 Kazakh elections, however, that the Russian population of the country was not being fairly treated, and amicable Russo-Kazakh relations cannot be taken for granted within Kazakhstan. A significant influence on Kazakhstan's future political orientation will be its relations with China. Increased trade and cooperation are possibilities; but so is a Kazakh sense of vulnerability to China's military strength, which would reinforce the argument endorsed by some in Kazakhstan that Russia should be encouraged to keep nuclear weapons there. In the longer term, President Nazarbayev's own position may be eroded, for instance by the possible rise of Islamic sentiment in his largely Muslim state.

Relations with Belarus

Aided by considerable sympathy for Russia's problems and a continuing Belarussian dependence on Russia for food, raw materials and energy, Russia-Belarus relations in 1993 and 1994 remained calm. A treaty on the coordination of military activities was signed but there was some dispute in Belarus about whether it should join a CIS collective security arrangement.[27] By early 1994 Belarus, with its economy in turmoil, was moving towards economic and security reintegration with

Russia, although not without considerable hesitation, and in June 1994 Alexander Lukashenko, on an anti-corruption, nationalist platform, looked likely to be elected President in the second round, having won 45 per cent of the vote in the first round. Prime Minister Vyacheslav Kebuch, favouring economic union with Russia, got only 17 per cent of the vote. Little therefore looks guaranteed even in Russia–Belarus relations.

Relations with the Baltic states

The situation in the Baltics, however, was much less reassuring. In early 1994 Russian relations with all the Baltic states remained unsettled, although slowly improving. The Baltic governments feel that the Russian authorities remain very reluctant to accept the independence of the three states. Ironically Russia is keen to demarcate borders, an important symbol of recognition, but the Baltic countries are reluctant to see this happen because it would imply that their claims for territorial adjustments had failed. Russia asserts a duty to protect not only Russians but also Ukrainians and Belarussians in the Baltic states and what it claims to be violations of human rights form a constant source of friction. Russia refuses to reveal the identities of its legal citizens in the Baltic states. On the other hand, the Russian Foreign Ministry points out that the Russian Federation actually helped the Baltics to become independent. It also presents in a reasonable form its three-pronged policy of support for Russian minorities in the region. The policy comprises:

* the maintenance of direct communications with Russians in Latvia, Lithuania and Estonia in order to be of practical assistance to them in adapting to new conditions of life;
* bilateral dialogues with the Baltic states; and
* the use of international organizations and contacts with leading countries of the West in order to draw attention to the situation of the Russian minorities.[28]

There was a clear military dimension to this problem. Russia was reluctant to withdraw troops from the Baltic states since they would have to leave significant military assets, officers would have nowhere to live in Russia, and units could be seen as protecting the Russian populations, including Red Army and KGB pensioners, in the Baltic states. However, the Baltic states were not prepared to compromise over their demands that all Russian troops should leave as quickly as possible, and Russia accepted that troops should be stationed in foreign countries only with the consent of the recipient government. In the event Russia did withdraw many troops, and Lithuania granted Russian forces transit rights across its territory so that they could reach their bases in Kaliningrad. In return, Lithuania was the first Baltic state to see all Russian forces withdrawn. By July 1993 there were probably fewer than 35,000 Russian soldiers in the Baltic states, and 15,000 by the end of the year (12,000 in Latvia and 3,000 in Estonia).[29] The final removal of Russian forces would solve many problems. The process should be facilitated by the early 1994 agreement, concluded with US support, which allowed Russia to keep use of the Skrunda space surveillance radar station in Latvia, manned by 500 Russian military and 200 civilians, for four years. It will subsequently be dismantled over an 18-month period, with the costs likely to be paid by the United States.[30] However, the difficulty of carrying through intergovernmental agreements among the successor states of the FSU was illustrated by the difficulties which this deal encountered in the Latvian parliament, where there were objections that aspects of the documents involved accepted as legitimate the consequences of the Soviet Union's annexation of Latvia. Some deputies wanted negotiations reopened, although they were eventually outvoted.[31] Russia, for its part, continued to worry about the fate of Russian military pensioners in the Baltics. Nevertheless, the signs in 1994 were that Russia would remove all its troops from Estonia and Latvia by the end of August 1994, save for those manning Skrunda.[32]

The political questions arising from the civil Russian populations of Latvia and Estonia will remain difficult. The Baltic states would prefer many Russian civilians to leave since they constitute a majority of the population in important parts of their countries: for example, there are more than 60,000 retired Russian officers in Riga but many other Russian inhabitants are younger. Narva in Estonia is a largely Russian-populated city. Estonia and Latvia are introducing constitutions which severely limit the capacity of people not speaking their native languages to become citizens, a development which affects most Russians. Under outside pressure these plans are being reconsidered, and it is possible that arrangements for Russians to receive temporary and later permanent residence permits may defuse the issue for the time being.[33] In general, Russian relations with Estonia and Latvia seem likely to be dominated by two variables, political developments in Russia and economic life in the Baltics. The more nationalist and intimidatory the government in Moscow, the less inclined it will be to accept the sovereignty of the Baltic states. The more there is economic advance in the Baltics in which the Russian population can share, the less Russians there will seek support from Moscow. It will be more likely that they will reinforce their attitudes of 1991 and 1992, when many of them supported the secession of the Baltic states from the Soviet Union.

The agreements of September 1992 between Russia and Lithuania on access to Kaliningrad and troop withdrawal did not cover property, compensation for environmental damage and so on. Implementation of the agreements is causing some friction as Lithuania objects to not being informed in advance about troop movements. Given the loss of their facilities in Latvia and Estonia, the Russian armed forces are keen that Kaliningrad should be Russia's main Baltic facility and continuing tensions can be expected over transit issues.

There are also formal Baltic territorial disputes. Russia formally recognizes the 1991 frontiers of the Baltic states but Estonia and Latvia both lost some of their 1920 territory when they were forcibly annexed by the Soviet Union in 1940. About 5 per cent of Estonian territory was involved, along with the Pskov Oblast and Abrena area in Latvia. Some members of the Baltic states' parliaments want these claims pressed.

Significantly, they also affect Russian–Japanese relations since there are some Russian fears that, if Moscow made concessions on either the Northern Territories or the contested territories in the Baltics, it would come under pressure to give way on both, given that both were seized during the Second World War. In principle, there could be links also with the Crimean issue. If Russia argued that the 1991 frontiers of the FSU need not be maintained and that Russia's 1954 transfer of the Crimea should be rescinded, this would strengthen Estonia and Latvia's case that other territorial adjustments made during the time of the Soviet Union should be abandoned. Clearly, Russian relations with the Baltics will remain problematic, and Ukraine and the Baltic states, feeling they face a common problem of Russian power, may be drawn closer together.

The Caucasus

The situation in the Caucasus region overall is daunting in its complexity. A mountainous area, recently described as 'a living museum of ancient races and a repository of languages, creeds and cultures', its northern part is in the Russian Federation whereas Transcaucasia to the south comprises Georgia, Armenia and Azerbaijan. Georgia and Armenia are largely Christian areas surrounded by Sunni and Shia Islamic societies, but all states and Russian regions in the Caucasus are ethnically diverse. The scope for conflict stemming from demands for local autonomy and rights, contested forms of government, and economic instability is immense.[34] Dagestan, a Russian autonomous republic, could be a source of particular difficulty, but unless Russia can keep control of the northern Caucasus, the whole region could fall prey to continuous conflict.

Even by 1989 extensive violence was already being used over Nagorny Karabakh, an enclave made up mainly of Armenians within Azerbaijan,[35] and that conflict remains unresolved. In essence, the Armenians in Azerbaijan seem likely to feel secure only if they acquire further territory linking them geographically to Armenia itself. This could then lead to its political incorporation within Armenia. Azerbaijan wants to maintain its territorial integrity but has lost considerable land to Armenian military forces. The notion that Armenians might live in Azerbaijan with their rights as a minority protected will not appeal to either party. Also the incidence of factions on both sides (including inter-Azerbaijani conflict in Azerbaijan) has made coherent action or bargaining by any party more difficult.

Elsewhere in the region Georgia was torn apart by civil war, with effective and violent separatist movements under way in Abkhazia and South Ossetia[36] until Russia intervened to bring Georgia into the CIS in late 1993. However neither the Abkhazians nor the South Ossetians are satisfied with the political arrangements prevailing in the spring of 1994 and further outbreaks of violence cannot be ruled out.

Moldova

The independence of Moldova could lead to its largely Romanian population choosing to merge with Romania in a single state, although opinion was not running in that direction in 1993[37] and in 1994 economic weakness and a pro-Russian election result led Moldova to join the CIS.[38] Union with Romania would not be an appealing prospect for the Hungarians or the 150,000 Gauguz (a Turkic but Orthodox group) in Moldova, or for the Russians and Ukrainians who make up over half the 650,000 population of the Trans-Dnestr region (with its two power stations supplying Moldova). In 1992 Trans-Dnestr, with the support of the locally based 14th Russian Army and Cossack volunteers, virtually seceded from Moldova. A ceasefire in July 1992 ended six months of fighting against the Moldovan government. However, Russia does not seem happy to leave its 14th Army in Trans-Dnestr for ever, and in the spring of 1994 seemed to be seeking its withdrawal, since 'peacekeeping battalions are needed in other areas'.[39] Moldova, for its part, could turn to claiming territories in Bessarabia handed over by Stalin to Ukraine, but as of early 1993 Moldova and Ukraine were both opposed to the Dnestr Republic. Ukraine did not want to see a precedent set which could help the Crimea secede, and it did not want a Russian Trans-Dnestr base on its southwestern border. In addition, the Ukrainian minority in Moldova was being well treated.[40]

In and around the FSU, many more republic borders do not reflect linguistic or religious divisions.[41] Poles in Lithuania, who comprise 7 per cent of the population, were the victims of some discrimination although there appeared to be no problems for the 300,000 Ukrainians and 300,000 Belarussians in Poland. A US army analyst has observed that, 'if left unrestrained, the political power of ethnic nationalism could easily destabilize each and every one of the newly independent republics'.[42]

Central Asia

Central Asia presented a particularly complex situation, as Hélène Carrère d'Encausse explained:[43]

> The complex map of Central Asia had been considerably modified, especially since the war years, by three elements, all involving population movements – a massive and continual dispatching of Russians to the periphery; Stalin's deportation of entire ethnic populations, from the Germans of the Volga to the peoples 'punished' for collaboration; and the final wave of refugees from the war in the Transcaucasus, for whom the Soviet government tried to find sanctuary.

Conflicts included civil war in Tajikistan, most recently between the forces of President Rakhmonov,[44] who were closely associated with the former communist regime and supported by Russian-officered units, and those who placed a greater emphasis on Islam and had backing in Afghanistan.[45]

In the longer term, possible dominance of the region by Uzbekistan could be resisted by other Central Asian states, particularly Tajikistan and Kazakhstan, while ethnic divisions, probably more than fundamentalist Islam, threaten the peace and integrity of all states in that area.[46] Internal and even international conflicts, especially in the Caucasus and Central Asia, could be exacerbated by the reduced economic resources which Moscow is directing towards its former empire. Even in 1992 Russian sources estimated that these resource flows in all forms, including subsidized energy supplies, cost $18 billion,[47] a much lower figure than earlier but nonetheless significant. Its eventual disappearance will put more stress on successor-state governments. Paul Kennedy has pointed to the possibilities for violent conflicts in Central Asia as a result of water shortages, pollution, rapid population growth and falling agricultural output. He compared the situation in the area with that in most of North Africa.[48]

New international relationships

In all, the break-up of the Soviet Union generated 22 new international relationships among geographically adjacent FSU states and a further 21 relationships among FSU successor states and non-FSU neighbours. The current Western hope is that these relationships will stay essentially cooperative, broadly because of the enlightened self-interest of the governments concerned, the commitments made by FSU countries in CSCE documents and the UN Charter, and the multilateral framework of the CIS which links several states. Yet some analysts see great potential for violence.[49]

By late 1993 there were growing Western concerns that Moscow was becoming more assertive in its own disputes and manipulating quarrels among others in a possible effort to recreate a version of the former Soviet Union.[50] Zbigniew Brzezinski has pointed to the appeal of imperialism for Russia and to the possibility that such an approach could prevent the disintegration of the country.[51] Yet, although the Baltic states and even Ukraine were clearly vulnerable to Russian military capability, and Russia had clearly interfered in Georgian and Moldovan civil conflicts to win influence and to press these countries into the CIS, there were clear economic and military limits on Russian power. There were fears in Russia that even the reintegration of Belarus with Russia would prove an unacceptable expense and certainly any effort to reintegrate Ukraine would be costly in both economic and military terms: crushing the nationalist sentiment of the Ukrainians in the west of that country would not be easy for a Russia where conscription even for non-dangerous duties is highly unpopular. Russia, like most of the West where small families predominate, is affected by what Edward Luttwak has described as a reluctance to wage war if significant casualties are likely or even possible.[52] In basic terms, even during the latter years of the Soviet Union, Moscow had trouble in controlling its empire. There is little reason to think that it would be better placed to control the Caucasus and Central Asia in the mid-1990s than in the mid-1980s. Moreover, the more attention and resources Russia needs to devote to its west and south, the more vulnerable it will be to Chinese pressures. It also still has problems with Japan over the Northern Territories issue and there were signs in 1994 that Russia regards the Asia-Pacific region as an area of both opportunity and danger.[53] In brief, since an assertive Russia would have its military hands full and its economy over-stretched by efforts to control the near abroad, it would be easy to over-state the dangers to the West of Russian imperialism.

The forms of international relations linking Russia and its neighbours and Russia and the West have yet to be settled with historical experiences, religion, ethnic rivalries, economic factors, and political cultures all likely to play significant roles.[54] There is some, but not overwhelming, evidence that Russia will be able to accept Ukraine and the Baltic states as sovereign entities and legal equals, and to exchange physical control for 'more foreign policy'.[55] However, there is recognition in Russia that relations with these states would be among Moscow's most important and difficult links and it may yet seek to deal with them primarily through threat and intimidation. Certainly Russia feels a sense of responsibility for international order in the former Soviet Union.

Economic confusion

An ambivalent element in the international relations of the former Soviet bloc is the extensive economic interdependence which had existed under the Soviet empire. From 1989, many trading/exchange ties were dislocated and in principle the restoration of exchanges could do much to enhance economic standards and to build cooperative habits among the new governments. In practice, however, the problems of high rouble inflation and of moving to world prices for goods have made difficult the re-establishment of trade and of a rouble zone. Barter and the dollar continue to be necessary for exchange. Moreover, Ukraine and the Baltic states in particular are not keen to rebuild economic interdependence with Russia, which they feel would enhance their political vulnerability. They want to build up economic ties with the West, and Estonia and Latvia are looking particularly to the Scandinavian countries.

In this position of political ambivalence and economic confusion, the CIS is not an institution which inspires enormous confidence, although by 1994 Russia seemed to be using it increasingly and to good effect as a means of influence. Created at the end of 1991, the CIS did not initially attract the Baltic states or Georgia and then lost the active participation of Azerbaijan. Ukraine was quite open in stressing it as a means of promoting the peaceful dissolution of the Soviet Union.[56] The Agreement on the Concept of Military Security of the CIS reached in Bishkek in October 1992 was signed only by Russia, Kazakhstan, Kyrgyzstan, Tajikistan, Uzbekistan and Armenia. The agreement comprised an analysis of the wider world, including a conclusion that 'the military threat to the Commonwealth will be hardly eliminated in the near future', a commitment in the event of a threat to 'put into action the mechanism of joint consultations with the aim of coordinating their positions and taking measures to remove the threat', and declarations of respect for one another's borders and sovereignty. Nuclear deterrence was to be assured by the 'Strategic Nuclear Forces of the Russian Federation' and collective observer and peacekeeping forces would be established to end armed conflicts within the CIS. The latter forces had not proved possible by 1994. Decision-making procedures involving the CIS Ministerial Council, and its working body, the 'Collective Security Council', for the use of 'Joint Armed Forces of the Commonwealth', were laid down and the duties of such forces were specified as including warning of missile attack. A Council of Defence Ministers was also established.[57] The Bishkek document, with its stress on joint armed forces, reflected the reluctance of Moscow military authorities to see all traces of former Soviet forces disappear, and the limited support for this view in the CIS as a whole. Few states had ratified the Bishkek document by the summer of 1993 and Moscow abandoned plans for CIS joint forces,[58] if not for a CIS command. CIS High Command arrangements continued to evolve and in 1994 it was agreed that non-Russian members would provide 50 per cent of the command staff, and pay 50 per cent of the costs. The Chairman of the CIS Council of Defence Ministers, a rotating position, was to supervise the CIS.[59]

When the ten states participating in the CIS met for a summit in January 1993, Ukraine, Moldova and Turkmenistan refused to sign the founding charter, although they signed a document stressing that they would stay part of the CIS. Even those which did sign (Russia, Belarus, Kazakhstan, Armenia, Uzbekistan, Tajikistan and Kyrgyzstan) left the agreement for approval and possible modification by their parliaments. The effectiveness of the central bank agreement element in the charter seemed limited, given Ukraine's non-participation. Ukraine and Kazakhstan reiterated their rejection of Russia's demand that it should immediately take over control of the nuclear weapons on their soil.[60]

The CIS continued to suffer from its association with the former Soviet Union and Moscow's dominance. One Ukrainian author tellingly quoted Ilya Glazunov, a Russian artist who had said 'For some it is the CIS, and for us – Great Russia'.[61] This perception of the way in which many Russians saw the CIS placed a basic limit on its potential, despite the cooperative success which was occasionally claimed for it. President Yeltsin and President Shushkevich of Belarus both praised progress at the Minsk 1993 summit and earlier the then Commander in Chief of CIS armed forces, Marshal Yevgeny Shaposhnikov, noted progress in military cooperation during 1992, which he presented as in the interest of the West.[62] But participating states seem likely to see the CIS as at most an element in their bilateral relationship with Russia and to try to take from it their specific needs, whether economic, political or military. Belarus will be keenest on economic cooperation (i.e. help), while Armenia will seek to win Russian support in its conflict with Azerbaijan. Ukraine goes along with the CIS largely through economic necessity, and thus in March 1994 took up associate status of the CIS economic union. Moldova and Georgia too have been pressed into the CIS. Members' readiness to contribute positively to the CIS seems modest and strikingly Russia is struggling to achieve greater CIS participation in the 'peacekeeping' operation in Tajikistan. Belarus in particular seems determined not to get involved despite Russian pressure.[63]

Competition for influence

Weakness in a society can also tempt others to seek influence. A competition for influence in Central Asia is already clearly under way, with Turkey and Iran both pressing their case. Saudi Arabia is also investing in the promotion of Islam in the FSU, while it is unclear how Uzbekistan will seek to use its relative weight in relations with its smaller Central Asian neighbours. Such competitiveness could lead to a deterioration of relations among the outside states and to confrontation with other states of the FSU. There was some merit in the observation that 'should the geo-political unity of the CIS collapse, the appearance of new points of confrontation is inevitable', involving a drive for influence in the FSU from the west (NATO states), the south (Iran, Turkey, Afghanistan and Saudi Arabia) and the east (China and Japan).[64] Most positively, the states of Central Asia could use the CIS as a means of managing their relations, of limiting the influence of outside countries, and of sustaining Russian interest in their region. Such interest cannot be taken for granted since, if Russia becomes completely reconciled to the loss of Ukraine, the traditional source of much of its food and coal and the most important part of Moscow's earlier domain, it could well lose much of its involvement with Central Asia, historically an economic burden for Moscow, especially if it abandons the fears of Islamic fundamentalism which have brought it into the Tajik conflict. Roland Dannreuther stresses that what is currently under way in the region is a process of gradual Russian disengagement from the region, and a slow integration of Central Asian states into their wider region – one that includes Turkey and Iran. Moreover, he asserts that the Central Asian states are truly sovereign and jealous of their standing: should Russia seek to dictate to them, they would react firmly, knowing that other alliances are open to them. 'Russia's respect for the sovereign rights of Kazakhstan and Uzbekistan, and to a lesser extent the three smaller countries of Central Asia, is an essential pre-condition for their cooperation'.[65]

The CIS could well slow a process of Russian disengagement and the southeastern thrust of the CIS could emerge as its most important direction. By 1994 Moscow clearly saw the CIS as its preferred means for tying former members of the Soviet Union to Russia, but such an approach in the long term could drain Russia of resources rather than add to its power. Russia could well find its Caucasian and Central Asian clients ever more demanding of economic aid and perhaps requiring a continuous Russian military effort, for instance in Tajikistan. There is awareness of this in Moscow, and Sergei Karaganov, one of President Yeltsin's advisers, has observed with insight, 'Now it seems there is growing consensus. Most feasible regimes in Moscow (except for a nationalist socialist one, which would try to force political integration) would probably attempt a modality under which CIS countries would remain independent politically but be dominated economically. No sane government in Moscow would choose to take responsibility for managing both the surrounding weak economies and their turbulent societies – as that would mean taking responsibilities off the shoulders of local leadership and free them to blame Russia for all their ills. Russia also cannot afford total separation, nor a policy of benign negligence.'[66]

In all states of the FSU, complete economic collapse and/or civil war remain real possibilities, although many old-style communists remain in power, particularly in Belarus and Central Asia. The consequences of possible broad civil and economic failure in the FSU cannot be easily assessed. If Russia or other republics fall into chaos and civil disorder, or if such disorder merely threatens, the prospect of a seizure of power by nationalist elements allied to the military cannot be ruled out. Once in power they could adopt a highly nationalist and aggressive attitude towards the outside world. Civil war, on the other hand, could mean the loss of control over the thousands of nuclear warheads in Russia, lack of maintenance at nuclear power facilities, and millions of refugees heading for East/Central Europe or Scandinavia and the Baltics.

Overview

The last three chapters have spelled out what needs to go right and what could go wrong in the security sectors of the successor states of the FSU, that is in the areas concerned directly or indirectly with armed force and armed forces.

It has been argued that the formal Russian military threat to the West has become ever more remote, even in the nuclear dimension. However, the potential loss of political control over nuclear (and biological) weapons remains a significant worry, as does the possibility of nuclear proliferation within and outside the FSU. In terms of military resources, there are many issues to be addressed if Russia and other former Soviet republics are to become democratic states with civilian control of the military sector and with growing economies. The conversion of most of the immense former Soviet military machine is needed. Finally, a series of disputes can be identified within the FSU which could involve the threat or use of force, or which already do so. The Russian-Ukrainian relationship is of key importance because of its impact on security in the whole of Europe. Implicitly, because of the lack of any significant apparent disputes, the security relationships between the successor states of the Soviet Union, on the one hand, and

Poland, Hungary, the Czech Republic, Slovakia and Bulgaria, on the other, should not prove too problematic. However, Romania's relationship with Moldova is a source of potential friction in Russian–Romanian relations.

Clearly this list of problems is not comprehensive. Many other issues which have to be addressed in the FSU could potentially acquire a security dimension. Debts need to be shared among successor states and repayment arrangements put in place; comprehensive economic reform is needed to halt declining output; effective uses are required for the Western aid available, democratization needs firmer roots, not least in the Islamic republics where outsiders are vying for influence; environmental clean-up issues must be addressed and further damage to the environment, particularly from nuclear reactors, must be minimized. The problems outlined here are simply those of rather direct security concern, and those which Western defence and security authorities may be able to help manage.

5 WESTERN INTERESTS, APPROACHES AND PRIORITIES

In the face of a daunting situation in the FSU, the West needs to specify goals, to set security priorities and to identify policy approaches to deal with both immediate and more long-term issues. The first four chapters here identified a mass of uncertainties and interrelated problems, and selecting from them must involve some significant judgments, particularly about the primacy of nuclear issues.

Western goals

Six key interacting and central Western security goals can be suggested with regard to the FSU:

(1) the prevention of nuclear and other non-conventional weapons proliferation within the FSU and beyond, coupled with sustaining the process of arms control and disarmament on the regional and global levels;
(2) the building and maintenance of cooperative relationships among the successor states of the former Soviet Union and among such states and the West. Real cooperation cannot be based on Russian intimidation and hegemony and must involve Russia's genuine recognition of the successor states as sovereign entities;
(3) the maintenance of a cooperative relationship with Russia at the United Nations on matters of international order;
(4) the establishment of sustained economic growth in the FSU, especially in Russia and those successor republics that have significant Russian populations;

(5) the further building of democratic political systems and liberal political cultures (including the subservience of the military to civilian authority) in the successor states of the FSU; and

(6) the maintenance of a Western alliance to generate Western solidarity and coherence on the range of problems arising in the FSU and to respond should Russia, perhaps under a nationalist/authoritarian government, once more turn to an intimidatory and expansionist foreign policy.

The first five of these goals relate to Western efforts to take full advantage of the cooperative security opportunities which have become available since the collapse of communism. The first three depict the cooperative nature of the international relations which would best serve the interests of the West while the fourth and fifth relate to the conditions within the states of the FSU which are most likely to promote such cooperative relations. Economic progress and liberal democracy in the FSU are not only desired ends in themselves for the West, but also the means to increased security. The sixth goal involves the Western need to prepare for the worst outcome as well as to work for the best.

The significance of proliferation and arms control needs little amplification. If nuclear weapons spread beyond Russian control, the global non-proliferation regime will be significantly weakened, the prospects for cooperative relations in the former Soviet bloc will be severely damaged, and the likelihood that nuclear weapons will actually be used in conflict will increase. Careful pursuit of arms control, for its part, can help to build cooperative security relations and to reduce one state's fear of domination or even invasion by others.

Harmonious, cooperative relations among the FSU states are a much preferable alternative to suspicion, rivalry and a pattern of power politics. The last of these would make it harder to get Ukraine, Belarus and Kazakhstan finally to give up their nuclear weapons. It would drive the states involved in conflict to search for outside help, thus drawing others into conflictual relationships in the FSU. Certainly in the Caucasus and Central Asia, Turkey, Iran and even Saudi Arabia would have plenty of possibilities for rivalry. The Baltic states, which anyway cannot easily be defended against Russia, would increase further their demands for security guarantees. The states of East/Central Europe would become alarmed as well as perhaps drawn into rivalries to their east and north. Poland, Hungary and the Czech Republic would certainly feel more strongly that they were in a security vacuum and would press even harder for NATO/WEU membership.

Given Russia's political development to 1994, granting such membership would strengthen nationalist feelings in Russia that NATO remained an anti-Russian body (and would present a whole new defence agenda for the West[1] – see Chapter 6 below). Refusing it with disorder rampant in the FSU would expose the limitations of the West and make more difficult the maintenance of order on an international scale through the UN and CSCE mechanisms. More widely, if aggression was allowed to proceed unhindered in the FSU, it would be much more difficult to raise broad coalitions backed by Western publics against future aggressors elsewhere, including in the Middle East. Finally, a pattern of conflictual relations in the FSU would make even more problematic the restoration among these societies of the economic ties which are necessary for economic recovery. The FSU successor states are unlikely to grow economically either on a basis of self-sufficiency or by trading only with the West. They need to trade with, and even invest in, each other.

Harmonious relations must rest on recognition of other states as legally equal sovereign entities, an attitude which Russia in particular will find hard to sustain. All the successor states of the former Soviet Union, indeed all states in the international system, need to be discouraged from defining their own security in terms which mean insecurity for others, and encouraged to take notice of the legitimate security interests of their neighbours. More effort needs to be made to enable the values endorsed in the 1990 Paris Charter to become deeply rooted among the political elites of FSU states.

On the global stage the West greatly values Russian cooperation in the UN Security Council. As daunting security problems appear around the world, for instance in Somalia, Angola, Iraq and the former Yugoslavia, the effectiveness and authority of UN resolutions are increasingly under challenge. However, one near-constant element of the post-Cold War world has been the ability of the Security Council to avoid paralysis and to reach decisions. The permanent members in practice have almost stopped using their veto.[2] A hostile Russia could change this situation fundamentally.

Such a development would not only frequently paralyse the UN, it would also make it much more difficult for Japan and Germany to play an active part in peacekeeping and peace-enforcing activities. By the beginning of 1993, both these states had begun to take part in UN peacekeeping operations and were moving towards policy changes, including probable constitutional amendments, which would enable them to take part in enforcement activities as well. Whatever constitutional changes are made, both states will keep a preference for UN-mandated military activities (as will other European states such as Italy and the Netherlands). The potential problems presented by a more aggressive Russia were briefly illuminated by Russian Foreign Minister Kozyrev's CSCE speech in December 1992, when he gave a presentation which could have been made by a nationalist, authoritarian Russian government, before retracting his words to the relief of all. As the *International Herald Tribune* then reported, 'With frightening suddenness the improvised international structure that seeks to deal with global crises seemed to be in peril of crashing down.'[3] Yet the more assertive Russia widely noted in 1993 and 1994 was still ready to cooperate with the West, as developments in former Yugoslavia in early 1994 signalled: for instance, in April 1994 Russia co-sponsored a UN Security Council Resolution ordering the Serbs to halt their attack on Gorazde and to withdraw. The resolution gave significant credibility to the NATO ultimatum a day later that the Serbs would be subjected to major air strikes if their offensive was not abandoned, which in turn led to a significant ceasefire.

The West therefore has good reasons to prefer a friendly Russia, but it must also be ready to live with the real possibility of a hostile government in Moscow.[4] Militarily a hostile Russia would not be a major disaster provided that NATO was maintained: by devoting a maximum of between 3 and 5 per cent of their GDP to defence, the Western countries could once more deter Moscow without seriously compromising their own economic prospects. Deterrence could even cost considerably less; however, there would be difficult problems to manage, in particular the absorption of a probable new flow of economic refugees, and as indicated, there would be hard choices to make. In particular, which countries would be given a Western security guarantee against Moscow-based aggression? Would Poland be welcomed into NATO? Would the Czech Republic? How would NATO strategy and force structure and deployments need to be changed? These questions are discussed further in Chapter 6.

In general, the goals listed above are complementary and do not need to be prioritized: selling nuclear weapons technology and furthering proliferation could not transform for the better Russia's or Ukraine's long-term economic prospects. Critically, provided that NATO does not act in a precipitate manner in terms of enlarging its membership, the West can guard against a return to Russian expansionism without provoking it. But one argument worth noting is that, if a choice is needed, economic growth should be given higher priority in the FSU than democracy.[5] While there are real problems in Russia associated with old industrial elites adding wealth to their previous power through the privatization of firms, successful economic growth can after all raise long-term pressures for increased democracy, as can be seen today in many parts of the Asia-Pacific region. Moreover, economic growth and cooperation can bring cooperation in other spheres. China is cooperative in the Security Council mainly because it wants to keep its access to Western markets and technology.

Significantly, the West now has a clear interest in a prospering and therefore potentially powerful Russia rather than in a weak state with a struggling economy. During the Cold War, if the technology transfer restrictions arranged in the West through Cocom (the Coordinating Committee for Export Controls) had the effect of holding back the

Soviet civil economy as well as its military capability, few in the West were much concerned. Today the position is very different. The combination in Russia and, to a lesser extent, Ukraine of nuclear expertise and weapons stocks, coupled with a large, impoverished, frustrated population including sizeable armed forces, could generate enormous disruption in the international system. For the next few years doing everything to make sure that nuclear weapons do not proliferate from Russia by one means or another must be a direct priority, but in the longer term such proliferation possibilities must be recognized as being linked to civil economic growth and political stability.

Then there is the question of whether it is in the West's interest to see Russia survive as a single large entity. There is no doubt that Russia's size and military potential will make it a difficult neighbour, but not one that is impossible to deal with, since its military and economic capabilities are likely to be limited. On the other hand, any process of Russian break-up would almost certainly lead to significant violence and disorder, as well as nuclear proliferation. Moreover, once a break-up began, it would be hard to control. The West would find it easier to live with an expansionist, authoritarian but controlled Russia than with a country disrupted by a civil war that would generate millions of refugees and leave thousands of nuclear weapons under limited control. That said, it is clear from experience to date with the former Soviet Union and Yugoslavia that the West cannot hold together a state which does not enjoy the support of many of its citizens. The most that the West could do would be to make sure that any problems of Russian civil disturbance were minimized for the wider world. Pushing ahead with nuclear disarmament as fast as possible, and ensuring the legitimacy of the Russian state by encouraging a better standard of living for its population would be paramount. The economic shortcomings of Yugoslavia were, after all, a significant element behind that country's downfall.

In the light of the problems presented by the former Soviet Union and the wider goals of Western security policy after the end of the Cold War, the West needs to avoid two extremes of fundamental thinking. One is the counsel of despair, which asserts that Russia is too large and confused for the West to be able to influence, that Russians must be left to sort out their problems for themselves, and that Western efforts should be focused on those entities, such as the Baltic and Central European states, which can be influenced and developed into democratic market economies. This might lead to the advance of chaos in Russia from which the West might suffer significantly. The other extreme line of thought concludes that Russia is a defeated state which can be engineered by the victors into a very different entity from what it was before, through the judicious yet decisive application of resources and political pressure. This line of thought ignores the fact that Russia is not a defeated state under occupation (unlike Germany and Japan in 1945), and is clearly often wary of outside guidance.

A middle line is to aim at the situation in the FSU being eased and managed in the short term rather than solved in any finite sense. Dealing with the security problems at issue will be a long-term affair, in many cases involving a decade. In this extended period, the West will have to risk the loss or abuse of some of the resources which it commits to maintain its insurance against things going very wrong in Russia. Despite this, the West can do much on an incremental basis to bring improvement. With this broad approach in mind, what policy lines and instruments appear to have particular merit?

Approaches and instruments

Initially, the established broad lines of Western security policy can be endorsed. Those broad lines consist essentially of the following points:

- Since NATO's London Summit in July 1990, members of the former Warsaw Pact (and their successor states) have not been defined as adversaries but have been treated as formally equal dialogue partners of the Alliance. From December 1991 the North Atlantic Cooperation Council (NACC) was the focus for discussions; and in January 1994 NATO confirmed that the standard 'Partnership for Peace' (PFP) agreements should lead to specific menus of cooperation being developed between NATO and the states of the former Soviet empire.

- 'East-West' arms control processes (the negotiation, conclusion and implementation of agreements) have been sustained. The CFE 1 Treaty was successfully amended to take account of the break-up of the Soviet Union, the CFE 1A agreement on troop numbers was concluded, and implementation of both was begun. Discussions on confidence-building measures have continued and agreements have been reached, for instance on the monitoring of territory under the Open Skies Treaty of 1992. At the nuclear level, disarmament has proceeded apace through reciprocating national decisions (on tactical and sea-based weapons) and through US-USSR/Russia agreements (the START 1 and 2 treaties). Global negotiations have proceeded, and led in 1993 to the Chemical Weapons Convention. In 1995 a review conference of the nuclear Non-Proliferation Treaty will be held.
- Emphasis has been placed on the value of CSCE norms as the means of shaping governments' behaviour towards both their own populations and other governments. The 1990 Paris Charter was followed by the 1992 Helsinki agreements giving a stronger institutional dimension to the CSCE, and confirming that all the former Soviet republics were covered by its agreements.
- Modest material and technical help is being provided by the West to aid countries of the former Warsaw Pact with their political and economic transformation towards stable, pluralistic democracies and market economies.
- NATO has been sustained and reoriented through the development of a New Strategic Concept and Force Structure. Its military concerns have been widened beyond defence of NATO territory towards peacekeeping and the range of activities which could be undertaken by the Combined Joint Task Forces envisaged at the NATO January 1994 summit. Efforts were made at

Maastricht and afterwards to strengthen West European coherence on security by constructing a more effective Western
European Union.

In building on these policies, difficult, sensitive judgments will be
needed regarding the FSU countries. One key judgment is that Russia
should be seen as by far the most important state in security terms. This
is because of its nuclear and conventional potential and capabilities, its
capacity to cause enormous disruption to European societies and
security on a global scale by descending into a terribly destructive civil
war; and its potential to help with the maintenance of order in the FSU
and in the wider world, not least through its UN role.

If Russia is the top priority, Ukraine must still rank highly, in part
because it has the agricultural potential and history to tempt Moscow
to seek to re-establish control, in part because of its potential to
promote proliferation by pressing again to become a full nuclear
weapons state, and in part because a conflict between Ukraine and
Russia would be costly and damaging for both. Except over nuclear
weapons, the West should try to avoid choosing between Russia and
Ukraine, since a policy which is too overtly 'Russia first' or 'Russia
last'[6] will provoke too much resentment. Although Kazakhstan and
Belarus are both significant for their disruptive nuclear potential, their
existing governments appear not nearly so suspicious or hostile towards
Moscow.

The Baltic countries have the potential to bring grave embarrass-
ment to the West since it would be easy for Russia once more to
overrun Estonia and Latvia in particular, and the West would be in no
position to rescue them as it rescued Kuwait. The immediate Western
and Baltic concern is that Russian troops should be withdrawn by
August 1994. But perceived unfavourable treatment of Russian minorities in these states could delay the withdrawal of remaining Russian
forces or even bring them back, as could the rise of a more aggressive,
militaristic government in Moscow which wanted the access to the
Baltic Sea that these states control.

In many ways the Caucasus and Central Asia are of less immediate concern to the West, but they have real potential to sharpen the Christian-Muslim divide. This would put pressure on the West, not least because of the stress it would add to relations with Turkey. Also, abuse of the significant Russian minorities in Central Asia could promote the rise of nationalist sentiment in Russia proper, but in 1994 the violent conflicts in Tajikistan in Central Asia and Nagorny Karabakh and Georgia in the Caucasus were being controlled without causing too many ripples in the world outside.

Preventing proliferation

Moving from countries to issues, nuclear proliferation is the biggest immediate problem raised by the collapse of the Soviet Union. The Western approach to date has recognized the need to address the problem of redundant scientists but the Science and Technology centres planned for Moscow and Kiev are making limited, indeed poor, progress. The Moscow centre could be fully operational by the summer of 1994 but it has been hindered by difficulties in the appropriate selection of both personnel and projects from the large number applying. Moreover, while the US and the EU have each pledged $25 million for the centre's operating expenses, and Japan has agreed to provide $17 million, Western aid has been slow to arrive because of bureaucratic procedures in both the West and the East which were meant to ensure that the money was properly spent rather than used in a corrupt way. Of the $800 million total authorized by the US Congress for nuclear disarmament in the FSU, only $25 million had been spent by March 1993, mainly because of Russian bureaucratic reluctance to cooperate on nuclear matters with the US, and because of US reluctance to risk the abuse of funds.[7] The overall position with regard to Western help on nuclear weapons by the start of 1993 was as follows:

- A $5 million programme to provide Russia with armour blankets to protect nuclear weapons was to be completed in 1993.

- Deliveries were imminent of accident response equipment to be used to diagnose damaged weapons, stabilize their packaging and assess radioactivity in the vicinity.
- Deliveries were due to begin at the end of 1993 of $20 million worth of kits to upgrade Soviet rail cars used for transporting nuclear weapons and material.
- The $15 million design phase was due to be completed in September 1993 for a storage facility for fissile material, which the US may help to build by late 1996.
- There was an intention to provide Russia, Kazakhstan and Ukraine with help in developing internal accounting and physical protection measures for nuclear materials.
- There was an intention to buy up to 500 tons of highly enriched uranium from Russia. That might cost up to $5 billion but no agreement could be signed until Russia agreed with the other republics on how to share the money from the sale of fissile materials from tactical as well as strategic weapons. The Russia-Ukraine deal of January 1994 brokered by the US could accelerate progress in this area.
- There was a multilateral programme involving the US, NATO allies and Japan with help in the establishment and operation of an effective export control programme, including licensing arrangements, enforcement, the transfer of international obligations into domestic law, and so on.
- There were plans to help Russia, Ukraine and Kazakhstan with the dismantling of missiles and the safe disposal of their toxic fuel. The implementation of these plans should also have been accelerated by the January 1994 nuclear weapon deal.
- There were plans to improve government-to-government communications links between Russia, Ukraine and Kazakhstan.[8]

Looking forward, Ukraine, Belarus and Kazakhstan need to be approached with significant carrots and a bigger stick in order to get nuclear systems off their territories as quickly as possible. Ukraine's agreement with Russia and the US should be accelerated in its implementation if possible, so that all nuclear warheads are removed from Ukrainian territory within two years.

Security and economic incentives to help these states to abandon any remaining nuclear ambitions are apparent. In 1992 the Atlantic Council of the United States issued a policy statement asserting that the US should 'take the lead in the UN Security Council permanent members' confirmation, collective and individual, that they will come to the security assistance of any state attacked or threatened with attack by another state with nuclear weapons. The commitment must be un-equivocal.'[9] Politically the January 1994 agreement outlined the stronger positive and negative security guarantees which the three Western nuclear powers and Russia would give once Ukraine met its side of the bargain and acceded to the NPT. China, looking to the 1995 NPT Review Conference, could give similar assurances which could particularly reassure Kazakhstan. Ukraine already has the benefit of the commitments to existing frontiers and the indivisibility of European security and peaceful relations which have been generated in the CSCE and underlined in NATO documents including the Copenhagen Declaration.[10]

Ukraine and perhaps others could at some point in the future argue a need for nuclear forces to fend off superior hostile conventional forces but this is a case which many states around the world could also claim, and one which NATO has long made and unfortunately has not yet given up, even in its New Strategic Concept. For NATO it is time to accept the strength of a different argument – that the only justification for nuclear weapons is to deter attack by other nuclear weapons and the imminence of conventional defeat cannot justify the mass destruction and unknown but lasting environmental damage associated with the use of nuclear weapons. A project led by Lynn Davis, since appointed Under-Secretary for International Affairs at the Department of State under President Clinton, has virtually endorsed a 'no first use' posture.

While the existence of nuclear weapons contributes to deterring any use of military forces, their central purpose in the future would be to deter the use of such weapons by others. Such a nuclear strategy is consistent with what has occurred politically and militarily in Europe. American nuclear weapons are no longer required to deter a major conventional or nuclear war. Americans will not lose their interest in helping keep the peace in Europe, if all their nuclear weapons are removed. On balance, the small risks that might arise as a result of these changes in the nuclear postures of Britain, France and the United States are worth the potential gains in preventing the proliferation of nuclear weapons in Europe.[11]

'No first use' is a much debated point which Western governments have been reluctant to accept. Nevertheless, it is one which the West should take on board, in part because it will help to lead Ukraine and others away from developing their own nuclear capabilities. Maintaining the present Western position (that NATO is entitled to threaten a nuclear response to deter conventional aggression, but that only the five established nuclear powers and their allies are entitled to such protection) gives support to nuclear weapon enthusiasts in Ukraine, in other parts of the FSU and in the rest of the world. This author believes that strategic ideas can be and are borrowed from one part of the world and applied in others, and has some sympathy with Brzezinski's premise that 'ultimately it is ideas that mobilize potential actions and thus shape the world ... Ours is the age of global political awakening and hence political ideas are likely to be increasingly central.'[12] In private discussions Ukrainian political analysts have already looked to the British and French cases to justify a Ukrainian nuclear capability. In addition, a Western 'no first use' stance would strengthen those in the current Russian debate who want to see Russia adopt a similar posture (which in turn could reassure Ukrainians), as well as in the longer term easing the political problems associated with expanding the areas of Western security guarantees, initially to cover Central Europe.[13]

Another encouragement to Ukraine to keep to its January 1994 commitments is that from outside it is hard to see how the security of Ukraine, or indeed any former Soviet republic other than Russia, could be enhanced by a nuclear weapons programme. A Ukrainian nuclear system would certainly further diminish Russian readiness to supply Kiev with cheap energy supplies and, in the purely military area, the key issue is not whether Ukraine could produce nuclear weapons, but whether it could deploy them in an invulnerable (probably mobile) mode at acceptable cost. Otherwise the system, like existing missiles and aircraft, would be wide open to a Russian pre-emptive strike, and would alarm Moscow yet not suffice to deter it.[14] Britain and France are well-placed to inform Ukrainian political elites on the costs and procedures associated with the deployment of even small nuclear forces. These arguments should not be forgotten in 1994 just because warheads have begun to leave Ukraine, since it is almost certain that Ukraine will have some second thoughts about a non-nuclear future.

The West must also provide, as Ukraine and Kazakhstan expect, economic rewards for giving up nuclear weapons and certainly the US, backed by Japan, has concluded that Ukraine should not incur costs in the process of nuclear disarmament. The US had offered Ukraine $175 million for implementing START 1, but President Kravchuk's visit to Washington in the spring of 1994 appeared to be marked by a doubling of US aid to $350 million. Moreover, a matching amount appears to have been committed for general economic aid, giving a total of $700 million.[15] This must seem a modest sum to Kiev, which had been seeking $5 billion as its price for nuclear disarmament[16] and is looking for $5 billion in aid for its energy industry alone.[17] When US Defense Secretary Perry visited Ukraine in March 1994, he added a further $100 million to US aid offers, half of which was for dismantling missiles, $40 million for industrial conversion, and $5 million each for nuclear material storage and export control.

To deal with the strategic missiles in Ukraine, the central tasks involved, for which the West will be paying, are:

- the removal of warheads from missiles, their transport to Russia, their dismantlement and the safe storage of fissile material;
- the removal of air-delivered nuclear weapons to Russia, their dismantlement and the safe storage of fissile material;
- the de-fuelling and destruction of missiles;
- the destruction of silos and the clean-up of the sites.

Ukraine had preferred that the warheads should be dismantled in Ukraine. This was not accepted by the West since it would have been costly and would have also involved the construction of specialist facilities which might in future have enabled Ukraine to build its own warheads. Strategic warheads in Ukraine are being taken to Russia for dismantling. Ukraine seems likely to be involved in the de-fuelling of missiles, the destruction of silos and the clean-up of sites, but the missiles will be sent to Russia for destruction.

The US is prudently providing a minimum amount of aid in recognition of Ukraine's nuclear policy changes and Western Europe, as a major beneficiary of Ukrainian disarmament, should also be willing to contribute. In the longer term, however, the West needs to scale its aid to Ukraine in response to economic reform there. Western aid needs to be sufficient to demonstrate concern for Ukraine and appreciation of its value, but there is clearly no point in supplying huge amounts of aid where there has been no privatization, reduction in government's spending deficits or wider economic reform. The West should signal a readiness to be generous with economic aid and trade concessions towards a non-nuclear and economically reformed Ukraine.

The West correctly set a harsh precedent with Ukraine in being unwilling to provide any significant help to a government which was threatening to go nuclear. The West's interest in preventing proliferation and discouraging Ukraine's use of nuclear weapons as economic levers justified such a hard line. Western interests would after all have been better served by a Moscow-dominated Ukraine than by a nuclear Ukraine in confrontation with Moscow. Moreover Ukraine's history of ambiguity and prevarication on the nuclear issue since 1991 means that major Western economic aid should be withheld until the warheads have been withdrawn and Ukraine has acceded to the NPT. This need not take long and in the meantime the close diplomatic ties with the West which Ukraine seeks[18] can be developed, 'to show Ukrainians that we value them as a distinct and independent nation'[19] and to reduce Ukrainian perceptions of isolation. Feasibility studies and provisional offers can be made by the West on such matters as infrastructure improvements, and technical help plans and loans can be prepared but withheld.

The line to be promoted is that Ukraine's size, location, history, economic potential and needs justify a significant Western aid programme but that preventing proliferation is the supreme Western concern. This means, it must be admitted, that the West must be prepared to risk political and social instability in Ukraine, following from economic problems, if Kiev withdraws its readiness to cooperate on nuclear matters. However, Ukraine is not being asked to accept a reversal of its position, merely to do what it has already said it would do.

The Western interest in preventing proliferation also means that attention must be paid to Russia where the operation of an effective government (as opposed to civil war) is needed so that control is not compromised over the 30,000 nuclear weapons involved. Provision must also be made to create gainful, meaningful employment, preferably in a growing economy, for those with significant expertise in weapons of mass destruction. This suggests that economic and other aid should be directed firmly to Russia, and that almost any effective government in Russia is preferable to no government.

For longer-term proliferation problems, further research should be promoted on dealing with weapons-grade radioactive materials, especially plutonium. In the meantime a major effort over many years will be necessary to guard the 100 tons or so of plutonium and 600 tons of enriched uranium which will be recovered from redundant weapons in Russia.[20] In any civil conflict of the future, the sites concerned could well be prime targets for capture by anti-government forces and one possible answer would be to buy weapons-grade plutonium from Russia, and to put it under the control of a strengthened International Atomic Energy Agency.[21] However, the Russian military would be particularly reluctant to hand such security-sensitive material to an international organization, although it has seemingly accepted the plans to sell highly enriched uranium to the US. The March 1994 US-Russian agreement to open up each other's plutonium storage sites at Amarillo, Texas and Tomsk for mutual inspection is thus to be welcomed as the beginning of an international regime on plutonium control[22] and as a source of Western assurance that Russian plutonium is being properly protected. The techniques available today for disposing of plutonium[23] need to be further explored and perhaps new ones sought. One suggestion is for the suspension of plutonium particles in borosilicate glass, and the storage of the consequent 'logs' in deep geological depositories.[24] Releasing fissile materials for use in civil power generation would cause a major disruption to the civil fuel market, even if the release were spread over a decade or so.[25]

Implicit in the analysis so far is that restricting Russian (or Ukrainian) conventional arms exports should not be a Western priority. Many Russian authorities see arms sales as a reasonable means of earning foreign exchange and Western criticisms of Russian arms exports are interpreted as efforts to destroy the Russian defence industry and to weaken Russia yet further. These arguments will have credibility while the West refuses to strengthen significantly its own arms export restrictions and while Western sales are much greater than Russia's in value.[26] In practice, Russian arms sales for cash are unlikely to be extensive because Russia's credibility in terms of its ability to support its arms over the long term with training, spares, ammunition and updating packages has been eroded by the political instability it has suffered. Also credit and financing arrangements play a major part in the contemporary arms business but Russia is ill-placed to offer further credit since so many of its customers already owe so much. Syria's arms debts to the FSU may total $12 billion, much or all of which may have to be written off before Syria will 'buy' anything else.[27] Finally, the performance of Russian arms in the Kuwait conflict in 1991 raised doubts about their technological effectiveness. The demand for Russian arms at best is likely to increase only slowly from the 1993 level of perhaps $2.15 billion a year, as more realistic Russian arms experts realize.[28] Overall, it is hard to understand why Russian arms exports should be seen as more of a problem now, when they are at a comparatively lower level than when many arms were supplied as aid or on vague credit terms. The US Defense Intelligence Agency has reported that arms exports from all the FSU were only $2.5 billion in 1992[29] and they fell further in 1993. In particular, if the arms export discussions among the permanent members of the Security Council could be revived, any individual case causing Western concern could be quietly raised. The West can also encourage Russia to continue to record its major arms deliveries with the UN Register of Conventional Arms by recording its own exports promptly and accurately. Lastly there are growing links between Russian and Western defence companies, with *Aviation Week and Space Technology* producing in 1993 a five-page list of joint ventures. Arguably the effect of these links, as they mature, will be to discourage Russian defence enterprises from exporting to pariah states and to lead them to export in accordance with Western norms.[30]

However, it must be noted that more alarmist interpretations are feasible. Steven Blank feels that Russia could export significant amounts in exchange for debts to states such as South Korea, that export controls are easing, and that defence ministry direction of arms exports could lead to the Russian military using such exports as direct sources of revenue.[31]

The important Western thrust should be that the Russian and Ukrainian governments especially should have effective control over their conventional arms exports and Western help should be given to authorities to minimize smuggling, through the strengthening of paper controls and customs services. Pressing a very restrictive export regime on Moscow could well lead to a situation where those with arms in their possession and needing to sell them, for example, defence factories and military units, were more inclined to disregard central government and to sell on their own initiative.

Strengthening cooperative relations

As a fundamental element in the development of cooperative security relations among FSU states, the West must seek clearly to influence Russia's own definition of its security and national interests. Of primary importance is reinforcement of the argument that Russian territorial integrity is not under threat from the US, any European power or NATO as a whole. Confidence-building measures, including military exchanges, formal declarations such as the Charter of Paris (even if they involve repetition of previous commitments) and implementation of arms control agreements all have a part to play in easing any sense of paranoia in Russia. Overall, the more Russia is integrated through military, political, economic, social and cultural contact with the rest of Europe, the less vulnerable it should feel.

However, President Yeltsin has suggested that Russia be given formal responsibility by the international community for the maintenance of order among FSU states. He claimed that 'stopping all conflict on the territory of the former Soviet Union is a vital Russian interest. The world community sees more and more clearly Russia's special responsibility in this difficult undertaking. I believe the time has come for distinguished international organizations, including the UN, to grant Russia special powers as a guarantor of peace and stability in the regions of the former Soviet Union'.[32] While the West must be ready to accept a significant Russian security role to its south and east, Russia should not be given an explicit sphere of influence consisting of the area of the FSU,[33] not least because this would encourage Russia to seek to dominate Azerbaijan's and Kazakhstan's decisions over the future ownership and pipeline routes of their emerging energy industry.[34] As Ukraine's hostile reaction to Yeltsin's initiative indicated,[35] such an arrangement would cause hostility in much of the FSU (and perhaps disillusion among Western publics). It could also put more of a burden on Russia than it was able to carry: as signalled above, while one interpretation of the behaviour of the Russian army in Tajikistan, Georgia and elsewhere is that elements in the army are unwilling to give up the empire, another perspective is that Russian units would become less keen on deployment outside Russia if they began to take serious casualties and had accommodation available at home.

By placing CSCE and UN monitors wherever possible, the West should look out for Russian forces deployed to provoke trouble in order to justify their presence or which concern themselves solely with the protection of local Russian civilians (in the summer of 1992 even Russian Foreign Minister Kozyrev accused the Russian armed forces in Moldova and the Transcaucasus of enhancing conflicts by the supply of arms).[36] Wherever possible, Russia should be encouraged to deploy its forces outside its territory with a specific UN or CSCE mandate and preferably working with troops from other states. Russian Foreign Minister Kozyrev and British Foreign Secretary Douglas Hurd have agreed that peacekeeping in the CIS should be accompanied by international monitoring. The West should not acknowledge the legitimacy of forces organized purely on the initiative of a few members of the CIS, although some Russian authorities want the CIS to evolve into a body which can generate peacekeeping forces.[37] The Hurd-Kozyrev formula is that 'the principles underlying Russian, CIS or international peacekeeping operations would need to include: strict respect for the sovereignty of the countries involved; an invitation from the government concerned and the consent of the parties to the conflict; commitment to a parallel peace process; a clear mandate setting out the role of the peacekeeping forces (which whenever possible should be multinational in character); and an exit strategy for the peacekeeping forces involved'.[38]

Most preferable would be for all international peacekeeping/policing activities on the territory of the former Soviet Union to be organized with an international mandate and preferably some participation from outside forces. Currently Russia predictably links these two elements. It denies that Russia should need an international, i.e.

Western-endorsed, mandate if the West itself is not willing to help with forces.[39] Scandinavian troops and forces from Europe's neutral and non-aligned states might be easiest for Moscow to accept in the first instance, and Russian forces could still be left with the leading role. Since Russia has sought without success to establish a multinational CIS force for Tajikistan,[40] and since it has accepted a CSCE mission in Nagorny Karabakh and Georgia, it may not be entirely hostile in practice to suggestions for sharing the burden. Sergei Karaganov, an adviser of President Yeltsin, has written that 'Russia will have to continue [to be] a local peace-keeper or peace-enforcer. To do this effectively and avoid becoming a militaristic state, Russia needs two conditions to be fulfilled. First her role as a peace-keeper should be legitimate; and second it should be part of an international effort – under the control of international organizations and constrained by international law. That would deter Moscow from unlimited use of military power and ultimately dangerous unilateralism'.[41] Fundamentally, the West cannot deny Russia a supervisory role in its former empire, especially if the West itself is unwilling to make a major contribution to the management of real conflicts and the maintenance of order there, but it can work to put Russian activities under some sort of international supervision. This has implications for the UN (see below).

To minimize Russian reasons and opportunities to interfere in much of the near abroad, the West could help to protect Russians outside Russia (and other minorities) by asserting five principles:

(1) A government has primary responsibility for its territory and its inhabitants. The state should be reaffirmed as a territory-based entity, while still having responsibilities for its citizens overseas.
(2) Governments should offer citizenship to all who have been resident in their countries for a substantial period, perhaps 10 to 15 years, who will swear allegiance to the country, and who have a modest but adequate level of local linguistic ability.
(3) In the case of people who hold the citizenship of two states, the state where they are resident should have fundamental responsi-

bility for their welfare. Dual citizenship should generally be discouraged, despite Russian pressure for it to become common within the former Soviet Union.[42]

(4) In addition to the individual human rights to which all are entitled, minority groups, defined in terms of language and/or religion, should also be protected by the scheme of group rights already agreed in the CSCE and the CSCE should pay more attention to the implementation of standards.[43]

(5) With (1) to (4) in place, no group could easily assert the right to use violence to secede from a state. The CSCE mission to Moldova in early 1994, which sought to resolve the Trans-Dnestr issue by advocating its establishment as a partly autonomous region of Moldova,[44] clearly sought to remove the Trans-Dnestrian justification for armed revolt.

The criteria for Latvian citizenship suggested by CSCE Commissioner Max van der Stoel appeared compatible with these ideas. He was opposed to citizenship being based on any quota system and said that it should be available to those inhabitants of Latvia who had mastered the fundamentals of the language, learned the provisions of the constitution and sworn allegiance to Latvia, and who had lived in Latvia for a number of years.[45] Clearly adoption of such principles would cause problems for some Western states, not just the United States, but it is plain that no asymmetrical CSCE area human rights regime, with one set of rules for the East and one for the West, would be acceptable.

Human rights cannot rest securely on legislation and international agreements alone. As far as Russians in the FSU are concerned, the West should promote two conditions as foundations for longer-term stability. The first is that the Russian inhabitants of a society, whether Estonia or Kazakhstan, should have a reasonable chance to earn their fair share of the national income. They should not be the subject of economic discrimination arising, for instance, from outside development aid being directed predominantly to non-Russian areas. The second is that, particularly with regard to Kazakhstan and Ukraine, there should not be too wide a gap between economic performance and prospects for Russians in Russia and those in other successor states. In 1994 the comparative economic stability of Russia and the dismal situation in Ukraine is a recipe for Russians in Ukraine to want either to secede, or to return to Russia, where they would need accommodation and jobs. These two strategic points are pertinent both for Western governments and for the successor states themselves.

Moving beyond the FSU, implicit in endorsement of broad Western policy to date is that expanding the list of countries with specific Western security guarantees – that is, widening NATO membership to include the countries of East/Central Europe – would not be helpful at this stage, given the fears and threats of the Russian high command, particularly about the introduction of foreign troops into the territory of neighbouring states.[46] For the moment NATO should continue as a coherent Western bloc, reminding Russian nationalists that their positive political influence in Europe could at most be very limited. But NATO and its members also can and should regularly reassert their commitment to acceptable international behaviour as defined in documents such as the UN Charter and the Paris Charter of the CSCE, which have been widely endorsed. Then, even without providing security guarantees to former members of the Warsaw Pact, the Western states could make it clear that economic and other sanctions would follow any serious violation of UN and CSCE rules. The West could also establish some military deterrent effect against aggression by simply leaving open the possibility that changes in military commitments could result from intimidation or aggression. For instance, it should be made clear in private that Poland and other Central European states might be welcomed into NATO if Russia moved against Ukraine.

In 1994 cooperative international relations, especially in the FSU, would not be strengthened by NATO taking in new members. Forces of irrational nationalism in Russia are increasing while many economic and social conditions in Russia are deteriorating. Such forces would be strengthened by a wider NATO membership and Russian reactions could be both wide-ranging and grave. Should NATO's membership change, Moscow could almost certainly scrap the CFE Treaty on the grounds that the fundamental circumstances in which it was signed had changed. This would take away the Western capacity to influence the military balance within the FSU and to benefit from the transparency which the CFE Treaty brings. Russia could retaliate by abandoning many of the arms control and disarmament agreements of the past decade. Most worryingly, Russian intimidation of the Baltic states and Ukraine would almost certainly increase, with Moscow arguing that, as NATO's area of influence moved nearer to Moscow, so Russia should seek to expand its area of control before even more lands could be drawn into the Western alliance. Also, alienating Russia over NATO would make it harder for the UN Security Council to deal effectively with global order issues. Finally, a premature effort to widen NATO could split and damage the alliance: one dismal but plausible scenario has NATO ministers agreeing to take in new members but the US Congress then refusing the subsequent treaty. Such a development would be tantamount to giving a blank cheque to those in Russia who favour the military intimidation of its neighbours. Towards the end of 1993 elements in the German government, especially Defence Minister Volker Rühe, were pressing for the Visegrad states to be brought quickly into NATO, presumably on the grounds that such a change would provide Germany with a *cordon sanitaire* and ensure it would not be on the front line in any future Cold War. But such a change would be premature and damaging to European security as a whole.

In the language of academic students of international relations, the West should adopt an idealist posture, opposing aggression and illegal behaviour wherever it occurs, rather than a realist position, according to which a response to aggression is needed only when a state's direct vital national interests are at stake. Only by such a stance can the West hope to discourage those in Russia who are drawn to the threat of force, without persuading such people that Russians are being singled out for special, discriminatory attention.

Such an idealist stance would also be in accordance, ironically, with the harsher realities of international politics. In the years after 1945 the West did not judge it worth a war to try to roll back Soviet power from Eastern Europe. Despite Soviet domination of Poland and East Germany, Western Europe was able to feel secure and to prosper. To define the defence against Moscow of Poland or Hungary in 1994 as a direct vital national interest of Britain or the Netherlands would be to fly in the face of recent historical experience and of economic and military reality.

But even in the medium term – five to ten years – the Western security community and the alliances it includes will surely expand eastwards and economic, social and political links between societies of the former Warsaw Pact and the West will increase. Such links provide the basis for credible alliances in a democratic age, since they ensure that the people of one country can empathize with the interests and problems of people elsewhere. The ideal way to expand NATO would be for new states to be prepared, within such a timescale, for European Union membership. Under the Maastricht Treaty EU members are eligible for WEU membership, and so new EU members could have a West European security guarantee with minimum controversy. There would then be time to persuade US opinion that it would not be wise to have some ex-Warsaw Pact states covered by a European but not a Transatlantic security guarantee because of the uncertainty this could generate, especially in crisis. There would also be an opportunity to prepare the armed forces and defence establishments of new NATO members so that they could fit smoothly into the alliance. Finally, by the turn of the century or soon afterwards, either nationalist and militarist forces in Russia should have abated under the impact of economic advance, or else Russia will be clearly an authoritarian state with imperialist aspirations which the West will have to counter and with which security cooperation will anyway be hard. The problem with this approach, which offers NATO membership as a by-product of the genuine economic and social integration of Eastern Europe with the West, is that currently the states of Western Europe, including

Germany, are not willing to make the economic adjustments and sacrifices needed to make it work. It would be hard to persuade the US Congress that the Americans should fight to defend Poland if Germany is not willing to buy Polish agricultural products, the sale of which would help Poland to afford reasonable forces for its own defence.

A difficult but significant question is how the West's policy towards Yugoslavia relates to its policy as regards Russia and to Western hopes for cooperative international relations in the former Soviet empire. It needs to be recognized that nationalist forces in Russia must have taken encouragement from what the Serbs as an ethnic group have been permitted to achieve. Serbs outside Serbia have been allowed to capture territory by force with the aid of Serbia proper. A recognized state, Bosnia, was virtually dismembered. The West must recognize also that it will have suffered a significant loss of credibility, since through the Security Council it has adopted contradictory positions, subjecting Serbia to sanctions yet seeking to be impartial in Bosnia and Croatia between the Serbs and their enemies. The West has also regularly adopted positions and then done little to implement them because of the costs and risks involved. It has recognized new states in an attempt to strengthen those states' new existence, but has done little to protect them when attacked. It has defined war crimes but done nothing to bring the perpetrators to justice, nor even had any clear idea of what this would mean. It has proclaimed a no-fly zone and watched aircraft fly for months before introducing enforcement, and defined safe areas which it was unwilling to protect.

This loss of credibility is very important but, in the case of Russia, the significance of possible Western economic sanctions cannot be overlooked. Serbia has shown the limitations of sanctions by its readiness to endure economic dislocation and hardship but Russia would be particularly vulnerable to the suspension of Western aid, food and technology. However, if only because of the possible loss of control over fissile materials in an impoverished confused Russia, and because of the possible numbers of Russian refugees, the West would not find it easy to impose comprehensive sanctions on Russia. Also, as Western investment and trade in the former Soviet Union grow, the West will itself become vulnerable to the effects of any sanctions imposed on an expansionist Russia. This reflects the broad consideration that the West can never expect to deal with Russia simply with a blunt stick, since Russian cooperation is valued not just in terms of economic opportunities but also over several global issues, such as the non-proliferation of weapons of mass destruction, restraint in the arms trade, the control of terrorism, and the functioning of the UN Security Council.

This has three implications for Western policy. First, while the political situation in Russia is so uncertain, the West should recognize that it may have to abandon much of what it invests in the former Soviet Union generally. For some oil companies, the amounts may be very significant if Western firms and the Russian government succeed in negotiating the agreements which would enable Western firms to revive the Russian oil sector.[47] This may involve Western governments increasing their underwriting of private Western investments against political risk.

Second, the West needs a capacity to apply sanctions as surgical rather than blunt instruments vis-à-vis Russia. It may be necessary once more, as during the Cold War, to control trade with Russia so as to ensure that its economy can be penalized but not crippled, since a chaotic outcome would damage Western interests.

Third, the West has properly relaxed technology transfer restrictions to Russia so as to optimize the chances of economic growth and democratic politics. But if things go wrong in Russia, the West needs to be able to restore technology transfer controls. Cocom was abolished at the end of March 1994 and a new body with Russian participation is due to be established to cover export controls to the developing world. Whatever the new arrangements, Western governments need to maintain up-to-date lists of relevant products so that they could if necessary restore partial controls on Russia.

Improving security relations: the role of arms control

Fortunately there has been no political acceptance of the intellectual argument that arms control should be abandoned now that the political framework behind the negotiations has been transformed[48] and because existing agreements will be costly to implement.[49] The ratification and implementation of existing arms control treaties, especially the CFE Treaty and the START 1 and 2 agreements, will generate a significant agenda for some time but there is also a need to press on. The West should promote the argument that arms control not only reflects political relations but can also help to shape them in a positive way.[50] Arms control and confidence-building measures could in particular have an impact on the emerging international relations in the former Soviet empire. The CFE Treaty left many Soviet successor states with higher equipment entitlements than they need or can afford. As states develop new armed forces, defence policies and military doctrines, there will be a need to ensure that these do not cause unnecessary alarm to others. The principle that conquest through surprise attack should not be available to governments, which won acceptance earlier in an East-West context, now needs to be established in an 'East-East' context. This would lead perhaps to agreements prohibiting or limiting force deployments near specified borders, increasing transparency to cover logistics bases and other activities not covered by the CSCE, adding surface-to-surface missiles to CFE-limited weapons, and further limiting military exercises. In some areas exercises may need to be limited to regiment-sized activities. In the Vienna Forum on Security Cooperation there is already discussion of greater openness in defence planning and further information exchanges may be introduced on defence budgets and procurement plans. There could well be some interest in these measures in the Clinton administration.[51] As noted, in confidence-building terms, the prevalence of ethnic disputes in the former Soviet Union means that a stronger and clearer regime in the minority rights area would be especially valuable.

It is in the context of such points that the Russian pressure to modify the regional sub-limits of the CFE Treaty should be addressed. As noted above, basically Moscow wants to be able to deploy more forces in the North Caucasus area and in the Leningrad military district than it did when the Treaty regional sub-limits were originally negotiated. Its arguments are that the Caucasus is now a front-line area of instability, and the forces which Russia is withdrawing from Germany and the Baltic states will otherwise have to be deployed around Moscow or in the Volga and Urals military districts: this will be very expensive because a suitable infrastructure will have to be built. In return for a change in the regional sub-limits, Russia could accept lower holdings in the Kaliningrad area.[52]

In response the West should not insist on the terms of the CFE being cast in stone, not least because Russia has in many ways already been very reasonable in accepting the refinements to the treaty consequent upon the break-up of the USSR. Also, Ukraine's own regional sub-limits on the deployment of its forces could be modified to give it greater capability to defend itself against Russia. A prudent Western line would therefore be to accept in principle that Russia has legitimate concerns. However, the West should undertake only informal, exploratory discussions which could illuminate whether Russia is seeking a largely defensive capability in the Caucasus or whether it wants enhanced intervention strength, and it could stress that formal negotiation of modifications to the Treaty should take place at a 1996 review conference. In the meantime, the West may have to turn a blind eye to any minor Russian violations of the regional sub-limits which may be discerned.

Arms control could play a particularly significant role in the Russia-Ukraine relationship. An element in the CFE entitlements among FSU successor states is that Ukraine was allocated significant forces (see Table 3 above). If deployed and carefully prepared, Ukrainian forces could in the long-term deny Russia a capability to overrun Ukraine quickly or even to invade it at all with any success. Ukraine was allocated 64 per cent of Russia's tank entitlement, 42 per cent of its ACV entitlement, and 63 per cent of its artillery entitlement. The corresponding figures for combat aircraft, helicopters and personnel are 32 per cent, 37 per cent and 31 per cent. While Ukraine will struggle in the short term to deploy its entitlement, in the long term it has a real interest in the survival of the CFE Treaty.

This, of course, has nuclear implications. The better able Ukraine feels to protect itself with conventional forces, the less interest it should have in the nuclear dimension. Moreover, if Ukraine's behaviour causes the downfall of one element in the East-West arms control regime, namely the START treaties, it is quite possible that other elements, including the CFE Treaty, the Open Skies agreement and other sources of reassurance for Ukraine, would be rejected by Russia as well.

In the Baltic area, an arms control regime, coupled with Western readiness to build housing in Russia for displaced Russian servicemen, might help to reassure Russia that it could give up control of the Baltic states without compromising its security, and might reassure Russia's neighbours as well. Demilitarization of the Baltic Sea has been suggested as a way of easing Russian concerns about air and missile attack.[53] Certainly participation of the new Baltic states in Western military exercises, even of a search and rescue nature,[54] must be handled with great sensitivity if Russian fears are not to be fed.

On the nuclear side, however, START 2 will not be the end of East-West negotiations, particularly if proliferation in the former Soviet Union is avoided and if Russian relations with the West become even more cooperative. It was advocated above that the West should endorse a 'no first use' stance. This could obviously be done unilaterally, although a coherent position from the US, Britain, France and Russia – all of which have long possessed nuclear weapons – would have a greater political impact. Another likely topic for consideration would be a further reduction of warhead numbers beyond START, on the grounds that a true minimum deterrent would involve at most 1,000 warheads.[55] Britain and France would have to participate in strategic disarmament talks beyond START 2. Abolishing ballistic missiles would be a further and drastic possibility.[56]

The argument that, while nuclear weapons cannot be abolished, they could effectively be taken out of world politics (as slavery was taken out of European imperial economies) will continue to be heard, perhaps most tellingly from possible nuclear weapons states such as Japan and even Ukraine. This could mean that readiness issues could be formally put on the international agenda,[57] as could an increased concern with inadvertent nuclear war arising from an accidental or unauthorized nuclear launch. The danger of such a development during the Cold War, owing to the launch-on-warning stance adopted by both Soviet and American military establishments, was perhaps greater than is widely appreciated and firm arguments can be advanced for moving away from a high degree of readiness. In September and October 1991, Presidents Gorbachev and Bush made a start by taking strategic bombers, 450 Minuteman 11s and 503 Soviet ICBMs off nuclear alert. The measures agreed by the US and the USSR not to target each other have a largely political impact but could have implications in terms of minimizing the consequences of any unauthorized launch. There could be agreement that all missiles, on land and at sea, should be deployed so that they could not be fired within 24 hours; this could be verified by the deployment of personnel and sensors at launch sites. For land-based missiles, the warheads could be removed and stored separately, thus requiring even longer for firing.

There could also be cooperation on crisis management issues, including improved early warning arrangements, and perhaps the establishment of multinational, East-West joint facilities which would monitor all launches. Early warning would be strengthened by a great-power reluctance to deploy stealth and anti-satellite system.[58] Fears of strikes crippling command and control facilities would be eased if the development of bunker-destroying, earth-penetrating warheads ceased.

To improve further the security of nuclear weapons, Russia and the US could cooperate to ensure that all warheads were fitted with permissive action links and all launch vehicles with coded devices for their use. Russia is already understood to have explosives aboard its missiles which would detonate automatically should the missile fly off course. These could be refined to permit missiles to be destroyed from the ground after launch; indeed, provision could be made for the (radio-controlled) disablement of storage sites, weapons and launchers in the event of their capture by unauthorized groups.

In the near term, ballistic missile submarines could be granted areas of sanctuary for their patrols. The Russians are already interested in the Sea of Okhotsk becoming such a sanctuary, a change which would have a significant impact on conventional force levels in the area. Beyond arms control, the question of cooperation on ballistic missile defence (BMD) might become more serious and substantive, depending on proliferation developments.

Russia and the United States have had preliminary discussions on BMD cooperation and Moscow's position, backed by the ten states of the CIS,[59] is that the Anti-Ballistic Missile (ABM) Treaty should remain in force. However, it is argued that the Global Protection System (GPS) proposed by President Yeltsin will not violate the ABM Treaty since the ban on national ABM systems designed to protect against large-scale nuclear attack will remain in force, and it will have other dimensions besides the technological. As a leading Russian arms control official has said:

> GPS, as we see it, is predominantly a set of political, diplomatic and other measures to counter the threat of proliferation. After we agree on the joint estimate of the magnitude of such a threat, measures to counter it will have to be developed. So far we see the necessity for the establishment of a multinational Early Warning Centre, which would monitor missile launches around the world, and provide real time information to all participants. Events show that it may also be prudent to have effective coop-eration anti-tactical missile capability.[60]

For a range of reasons, the West can expect to proceed better with BMD, should it choose to go down that route, if it has the cooperation of Russia and Ukraine. Both have technologies which could enhance or undermine BMD efforts, and a specific cooperative effort to develop defences against Scud missiles is already being explored.[61] However,

Russian and US negotiators did not find it easy in 1994 to make progress on what sort of anti-missile defences should be allowed under the ABM Treaty. Russia is primarily interested in defending its own territory using large, immobile radars, whereas the US is also concerned to defend troops deployed outside the US by developing mobile radars and high-speed interceptors. The US is also more interested in defending against longer-range (3,000 kilometres and above) missiles which North Korea is developing and might export. Such missiles have higher re-entry speeds compatible with those of submarine-launched ballistic missiles (SLBMs) that are counted as strategic under START, and Russia is wary of a US capability which would erode the effectiveness of Russia's SLBMs.[62]

Russia and global order: the United Nations

To have a chance of managing security issues in the wider world, the West needs Russian cooperation on the UN Security Council. The West needs to accept two uncomfortable points in this respect. First, the established formulas for calculating Russia's financial obligations to the UN regular and peacekeeping budgets oblige Russia to pay much more than it can afford, given the disruption to its economy. Two alternative responses are feasible. One is to review the formulas so that Russia is asked for less. The other is to turn something of a blind eye to Russian debts in the expectation that, once the economy is reformed, and raw material and energy exports increase, Russia will again be able to pay its dues as a permanent member of the Security Council. Given Russia's sensitivity over its continuing great-power status, the second option is the most sensible, at least for the time being. Clearly Russia's failure to pay off its arrears is predictable and should not be used as an excuse for the US to do likewise. Second, Russia could increasingly link supportive votes on Western-sponsored resolutions to economic favours in other fields. China at least implicitly already pursues such a line and Russia's economic position is at best stagnant at a low level.

However, a more positive point is that by seriously involving the Russian delegation in New York early in Security Council consultation procedures the US, Britain and France in particular can reinforce a Russian sense of prominence in that body. Both during the Kuwait and the earlier Yugoslav crises the Western permanent members were intent on coordinating their own positions before approaching the Russians and then the Chinese. Such an approach should not be developed to the point where the Russians felt marginalized. They clearly felt resentment at their exclusion from decisions taken in early 1994 on air strikes against Serbia, and ways need to be found to involve Russia in difficult but urgent UN decisions about the use of force.

The West should be particularly sensitive to Russian signals accepting UN involvement in conflicts in parts of the FSU. As noted, while there are some, especially in the Russian armed forces, who see the stimulation of conflict in the FSU as a way of generating Russian involvement and thus bringing renewed Russian control, others in the Russian government are anxious to see the burden of handling FSU disputes spread among a wide range of countries. The West must be willing to play its part in promoting the anti-imperialist forces in Russia by being ready to make UN attention and resources available for the FSU, difficult though this may often be. Although in practice the CSCE might often be the body whose peacekeeping role in the FSU Russia as a whole finds it easiest to accept, the UN should not be allowed to evolve as a body which takes little interest in the FSU. Unfortunately, because of financial pressures and a lack of interest on the part of many UN members, there is a real danger that Russia will come to view the UN as irrelevant to its security needs. Regrettably the UN could not send a peacekeeping force to Georgia because it judged that it would not have the consent it felt it needed from all the parties, especially the Abkhazians. Only a small UN observer force proved possible.[63]

However, another aspect of the UN is the degree of reliance the West should place on it for world order management. Since a hostile Russia remains possible and would make the effective operation of the

Security Council as difficult as during the Cold War, Germany would be unwise to tie itself prematurely in its constitution to being unable to act militarily outside the NATO area without a UN or a CSCE mandate. It would be far more prudent to establish a constitutional capability to judge each situation on its merits and to act accordingly, albeit with a clear policy preference for an international mandate. This would be similar to the current Dutch stance. Intervention activities would, in the event of Security Council paralysis, have to be justified much more on Article 51, which provides for the right of self-defence (and the right to ask others for help). Russia stresses the right of CIS governments to ask for aid (most obviously from Moscow) as a legitimate justification for Russian intervention.

Economic development

Most of these comments presuppose continued improvements in Russian-Western relations and the stability of the political system in Russia. In this connection, while the Russian population 'may be cleverer than the intelligentsia thinks'[64] in terms of its readiness to tolerate temporary though real hardships, much will depend on the Russian capacity to institute steady economic advance. Some argue that only the smaller states in the FSU can be influenced or helped by the West, while Russia is too large and 'enigmatic' to be influenced from outside.[65] Yet simply monitoring developments in much of the FSU is not an appealing option for the West and Stephen Van Evera is among those who advocate that the provision of economic aid (based on specified political rather than economic conditions being met) should be at the centre of Western security policy towards the FSU. He argues that aid should be provided as a reward for peaceful behaviour, which he defines as having seven elements: the renunciation of the threat or use of force; robust guarantees for individual and minority human rights; acceptance of current national borders or of only peaceful means for their amendment; a readiness to adopt democratic government; commitment to the honest teaching of history in schools and the renunciation of 'nationalist, chauvinist, or hate propaganda'; the adoption of free market economic policies and the renunciation of beggar-thy-neighbour policies with other Eastern states; and cooperation with Western efforts to consolidate safely the former Soviet nuclear force.[66] He cites an aid figure for the FSU of about $100 billion spread over four years. Van Evera's argument is that the West's economic leverage is the best way of securing desired behaviour from governments in the FSU, a slightly different point from the view that violence and conflict are more likely to be produced in an environment of economic desperation and social dislocation.[67]

Despite the difficulties involved, converting defence factories in order to increase their civil goods output should be a priority, given the size of the defence industrial sector and its need for either orders or subsidies.[68] While all Western aid which encourages foreign and domestic private investment in Russia and Ukraine will facilitate conversion in some form, most obviously by encouraging the already significant movement of labour out of defence firms into the wider economy,[69] direct involvement with defence enterprises is also needed, and has begun to occur: 'By late 1992, there were 180 joint ventures involving organizations of the Russian defence complex, and 220 for the whole of the US'.[70] It is to be hoped that many Western firms and governments will take a serious interest in the 29 Russian state enterprises, many with extensive defence interests, listed by the US Department of Commerce in 1992 as seeking foreign investment, partners or cooperation.[71] Economic advance in Russia and elsewhere needs initiative from both local populations and the West, but Western firms should be encouraged by the governments to look for long-term relationships in the CIS, and not merely to make short-lived 'raids' in order to acquire particularly juicy bits of technology. The Westinghouse links with Russia, backed with modest funding from the US Trade and Development Agency, which should bring US software and computers together with Russian radar technology to improve Russian civilian air traffic control systems, could prove to be a model for others to imitate.[72]

A particular focus for Western governments, as opposed to companies, should be the efforts needed in particular regions of concentrated defence production, such as St Petersburg and specialized defence cities in Russia, Kharkov in Ukraine and Minsk in Belarus. Understandably, given its regional concerns within the EU, the European Commission is showing a particular concern with regional approaches.[73]

At the plant level, ex-defence production facilities need not produce goods which could compete with advanced Western products, so long as they provide reasonable value-for-money goods, preferably in a competitive environment where they do not possess a monopoly. However, identifiable products which can be sold in the West are particularly useful as sources of foreign currency for further investment.[74] Key qualities in any product need to be defined, with minimum environmental damage, reliability and ease of maintenance being near the top of most lists. Clearly, within limits, there could be less concern about minimum size and noise levels (in goods such as refrigerators, washing-machines or cars). Western companies and Russian authorities could pay more attention to Chinese success in converting some of its defence industry in a country where there was a known shortage of many goods.[75]

Western government money can still be used effectively in small amounts, as in the case of the $65 million from the US for nuclear conversion programmes for Russia and the other strategic missile republics. US businesses can be given modest, seed-money contracts of $1–5 million to develop pilot conversion projects.[76] In the longer term, however, there should be a demand for larger-scale Western government help, particularly to underwrite major investments associated with conversion.

Manufacturing is complex but its broad needs are well understood. It starts with design and specification of the product in the light of understanding demand. Many Russian firms have poor access to market information. Manufacture needs to be planned and managed through in-plant operations and sub-contracting. Attention has to be paid to capital investments and human resources. Marketing and distribution constitute the last formal stage. All operations have to be financed, costs calculated and cash flows controlled; all these are further areas of CIS weakness. Finally, and of crucial importance, systems need to be in place for product improvement and development, for making manu-facturing and other processes more efficient, and for the generation of new products. Western companies and Russian factory managers need to look at the assets over which they have control with these considera-tions in mind, and must be helped to fill gaps in their capabilities.[77] Manufacturing entities need product licences and marketing teams as well as finance. This means that the welcome relaxation of Western technology controls to the FSU should be continued.[78]

The West must facilitate the flow of technologies such as computers, telecommunications, and electronics in East/Central Europe and the former Soviet Union. It will be impossible for these nations to join the modern world or even to stand on their own, unless they are given access to the technologies that will enable them to develop the essential infrastructure and manufacturing base.[79]

The chief Western concerns should be, as noted, to keep the capability to restore controls. Also, the West must be wary of the possible unauthorized re-export of dual-use technology and so contin-ued efforts need to be made to help FSU states to establish and reinforce their own export control machinery. The West should be ready to accept some risks, as it already does when it sells to non-former communist states with poor export control systems. Moreover, easing technology transfer restrictions should not be linked to securing other forms of economic advantage for Western firms:[80] the West's security interest, especially in a successful Russia and Ukraine, is too important to be risked for commercial gains.

There are three further security-related points in the economic sphere. First, Western economic guidance and its systems need to build credibility by demonstrating success somewhere in former communist Europe. Politically, however, it would be most valuable for the economic corner to be turned first in Russia and then Ukraine where the potential political-military problems for the West are greatest. The

Czech Republic and Poland may offer the best immediate prospects in the former Soviet empire as a whole but politically it is desirable that national output in Russia, Ukraine and elsewhere should begin to rise again soon, preferably from 1994.

Second, there is more urgency for economic advance than for the establishment and reinforcement of formal democratic systems. A democratic system accompanied by economic disaster has poor prospects. To put it baldly, without steady economic growth in Russia a security system in Europe based on cooperation rather than confrontation will probably not be possible. Politically, as van Evera has indicated, the West must oppose firmly any effort to re-establish in Russia the sort of totalitarian state which left the former Soviet citizens so vulnerable. By 1994 Russia had a flawed democracy but the change with the past was enormous: ending a six-year stint in Moscow a prominent Western journalist wrote that under the USSR for all citizens 'defencelessness was all-pervasive. Even members of the Politburo were not immune ... Now the concept has almost entirely gone, at least in politics. People can say what they like, meet whom they like, marry whom they like. It has happened so fast and so suddenly that most young people can hardly imagine what it was like in the old days. The change is huge, yet unfortunately the victory is not complete. For many Russians defencelessness has transferred itself to the economic field.'[81] Thus the West should be content with the steady strengthening of liberal political cultures, where internal security organizations have a minimal impact on people's lives, where people feel able to think and speak freely and have access to a wide range of literature. As one Russian put it, 'The formation of democracy in Russia is a long process ... the most important thing is the *direction* of the development of the political situation.'[82]

Third, although the West could clearly be condemned for providing too much aid and treating Russia as a Third World state, and although there has been a real problem with the abuse and diversion of aid, the West should provide sufficient aid for the majority of Russians to perceive that the West would like to see their country recover and grow. Actual aid levels, as opposed to sums promised, have not reached this level. There is a significant perception that Western assistance to build a Russian market economy has so far been too little and tardy. In early 1993, of the 71 projects approved by the European Bank for Reconstruction and Development (EBRD), only eight were in Russia although several large projects costing $5.5 billion in all remained under discussion. Less capital had been committed to Russia than to Romania and the Czech and Slovak Republics.[83] However, the 1994 IMF decision to grant Russia a further $1.5 billion loan should encourage further aid and investment flows and the EBRD with Jacques de Larosière as its new director is much more ready to fund investments in Russia.[84]

The civilian and democratic direction of FSU armed forces

The Russian armed forces are the direct successors of the Red Army. The continued appointment of a general as Russian defence minister symbolizes how far the armed forces are from civilian control and the West must accept that transforming their culture will take a long time. This means building up a multi-level dialogue with Russian officers so as to influence their world views over the long term. A variety of means are available for this dialogue, including bilateral goodwill exchanges, talks on arms control and confidence-building measures, training programmes, joint exercises and of course all the activities of the NACC (see Chapter 6) and Partnership for Peace (PFP). Russia eventually signed a PFP agreement in June 1994. The continuous and planned spate of joint sea and land exercises between Russia and the West needs careful monitoring to assess the results, for instance in terms of the political and social contacts made between officers. The objections to US ground forces in Russia, which caused at least delay and perhaps cancellation of some US–Russian planned exercises, shows the sensitivity of these activities to Russian nationalists,[85] who fear the security risks from the presence of 200 US troops in a sensitive Russian area. The human gains from such exchanges, however, could well exceed the value of militarily facilitating Russian-Western operations most obviously in peacekeeping. Russia seems particularly to want help with the effective professionalization of its forces.[86] It also has a clear idea of what it would like from PFP, reportedly wanting to pursue four themes: defence conversion, political consultation procedures, military contacts and joint training exercises.[87] Yet guidance on civilian and democratic supervision and control must also be sustained by the West as legitimate agenda items. Unfortunately the West does not have a clear idea of best practice in terms of procedures for the civilian supervision and management of procurement, the role of parliaments in defence policy, and the political control of armed forces. Further Western consultation on such topics may be helpful as a prelude to stronger messages to former communist states about how they should direct their military. The Western emphasis on such matters should be on the practicability and advantages for the military of civilian involvement.

Joint operations also could be a helpful way of building direct relationships between the West and the armed forces of the states of the FSU. These could most obviously take place in the context of UN peacekeeping or policing missions. Already in former Yugoslavia Western, Russian and Ukrainian armed forces are involved, but such joint operations could work better if more preparatory funding was available for advance discussion and some re-equipment of Eastern European forces,[88] most obviously in the communications area. Efforts should be made to ensure that such activities enhance understanding of Western senses of political accountability, civilian control over forces and so on.

Russia and Ukraine could emerge as significant sources of peace-keeping/policing troops in the longer run (if the CIS does not absorb all Russia's troops). After all, they have a large stock of professional soldiers who need employment and who have access to basic equipment. The rates allowed by the UN more than cover the costs of a Russian or Ukrainian soldier and, with the end of the Cold War, many political constraints on the use of such forces have disappeared. Of greatest significance, the world is increasingly short of peacekeeping forces as the demand for them outstrips the supply. Western training help to Russia and some other republics could therefore include extensive guidance on peacekeeping operations – training which Canada, for instance, is well able to provide. However, it is vital that all UN forces should possess professional integrity, a matter to be monitored with care in the light of the rumours that Russian and Ukrainian forces in UNPROFOR could easily be 'persuaded' to allow goods through to Serbia in violation of UN sanctions and have been openly sympathetic to Serbian forces.

Risks and Western insurance

In all these aspects of policy, the West will have to take some risks; these must be faced and, in a controlled way, accepted. The first and most obvious is that economic investments may be lost, either because projects fail in business terms or because of political instability. As noted earlier, because of the importance of Russia and Ukraine in particular, Western governments should be more willing to underwrite investments in these countries than in others.

The second risk is that the West will be pressed towards paying too high a price for Russian votes in the Security Council, or for Ukraine, Belarus and Kazakhstan to give up their nuclear weapons, or for former Soviet nuclear weapons scientists not to market themselves globally. There can be no firm guidelines here, except that the West should never lose sight of the problems which proliferation would bring, and that it may well be dealing with near-desperate governments and individuals. Western governments must constantly bear in mind what they have already saved in reduced defence spending as a result of the end of the confrontation with Moscow.

A third risk, indeed a necessary consequence, is that by providing help to industry in the FSU, the West will create successful competitors in the global markets of the future, causing some disruption in the West. Certainly some industrialists in parts of the FSU find it hard to believe that the West wants Russian industry to succeed, and there may indeed be economic penalties for the West in specified areas where Russia or some other republic may have specialist capabilities. The West European and American satellite launch industry may well suffer significantly from Russian competition.[89] At the opposite end of the technological scale, in the spring of 1993 the EC was resisting the import of fish and uranium cake from Russia, ironically at the same time as floating the idea of a Russian free trade agreement with the EC which would give Russia better access to the Community than that enjoyed by the prospective EC members of Central Europe. The West will presumably worry less about buying, for instance, Kazakh copper, lead and zinc, although traditional Western suppliers in Africa and elsewhere may suffer.

However, the penalties for the West of economic failure in many parts of the FSU will be greater than the burdens of dealing with success. The growth of privatization and a market system in Russia, plus eventual Russian membership of GATT, could reduce Western fears about Russian prices and give Russia some of the market access it desires. Moreover, in the aerospace sector in particular, the West is in a position to help Russia and other republics serve the FSU rather than the global market and the joint deals with Ukrainian and Russian enterprises which Western firms are making will sometimes be the only way they can make sales in the FSU market. In addition to the deal announced in January 1993 between Eurocopter and three Russian helicopter companies,[90] many other Western aero-engine, avionics and airframe companies have signed deals with Russian groups to get access to the Russian market.

A fourth risk is that the West may transfer dual-use technology to Russia as part of economic support activities and then see that technology used for military purposes, since Cocom's controls have been reduced and abolished. At a meeting of Cocom, neutral and former Warsaw Pact states in late November 1992 it was agreed that the trade in strategic (dual-use) goods could be further eased if purchasing states had adequate export control procedures of their own, used goods only for civil purposes, provided accurate statements of where goods were going, and accepted on-site inspections when requested by the supplying country.[91] With national export controls still in place, these conditions presumably still apply and every reasonable effort should be made to prevent abuses of technology. But there should not be too much surprise or alarm if some abuses occur. Many Russian enterprises will be desperate and will seek to improve their defence products with Western technology, if only to strengthen their export prospects. Some organizations are of course already doing this legally, for instance with trainer aircraft. Fundamentally, the West's technological lead in defence overall now seems significant, although Western analysts are impressed by systems such as the SU-27 and the T-80 tank, and by the ingenuity which went into them. Certainly Russia does not have nearly the conventional strength of the former Soviet Union, and understandably will want to strengthen the technological capabilities of its armed forces after the humiliations of recent years. The central Western interest is that Russia should refrain from using its military force, rather than that it should not have well-equipped forces. Even a weakened Russia is much stronger in military terms than any of its neighbours and a slightly stronger Russia will not be additionally tempted to use armed force simply by its increased strength.

Ultimately the West's best insurance against deterioration in the FSU is the Western alliance system. The continued existence of a healthy NATO both ensures protection for its members and guarantees that even a hostile Russia could not dominate Europe. The challenge for NATO in future is to help with the continued positive transformation of states in the FSU without alarming Russia. As of 1994 it had done an excellent job but the task is far from over.

This chapter has covered a wide range of goals and instruments which are clearly interrelated, and it has sought to articulate some fundamental elements of policy. But how should Western policies be directed and harmonized, and what roles should be played by which international organizations? There is scope for national activity but clearly there needs also to be coordination and the West is committed to a multilateral approach in security matters. Thus the next chapter addresses the institutional implications of what has been said so far, paying particular, but not exclusive, attention to NATO.

6 THE INSTITUTIONAL DIMENSIONS OF WESTERN POLICY

Whatever the nature of Western policies towards the territories of the FSU, they need to have a collective, coordinated character if they are to be effective. The coordination must be across countries by topic – that is, Western states should have a common approach to the nuclear proliferation issues; and also across topics, so that, for instance, Western policies on the regeneration of the Russian economy must take security considerations into account. As the previous chapters showed, there are many intrinsically linked issues in the FSU. This poses major challenges for Western governments which, despite institutions such as NATO, the EU and the WEU, still often deal with security policy on a unilateral basis.

In this complex situation, the role of international bodies as coordinators and perhaps initiators of Western action assumes great importance, yet Van Evera has noted that even on the economic side 'the West lacks an agency for taking unified action towards the East. The G7 are the logical group but there is no secretariat. [Cocom] has the most appropriate membership, but the wrong staff'.[1] In the security field alone, there are several relevant institutions, although all of them have other concerns besides the FSU and most were established to deal with threats arising from the Cold War. What can be said specifically about NATO, the body which traditionally was at the centre of the West's security relationship with the former Soviet Union?

Of initial note is that, of the six targets noted at the beginning of Chapter 5 for Western policy towards the FSU, only one, the continued maintenance of an alliance in case Russia should turn once more into an aggressive state, involves NATO as the primary player. However, along with other bodies, NATO could also make a major contribution to cooperative relations in Europe, to economic progress through its concern with defence resources and industries, and to democracy in the FSU if it could help with the introduction of civilian control and democratic supervision of defence activities.

NATO's defence role

Evidence in the first two chapters made clear that NATO's defensive duties should not yet be abandoned. NATO's defence planning must take account of two extreme contingencies, as well as intermediate situations. One is that Russia's orientation towards cooperation will increase. The other is that it will revert to an intimidatory stance, relying predominantly on military strength to further its perceived interests. Such a Russia might move quickly to re-establish control over the Baltic states, Belarus and particularly Ukraine (whose loss was felt most keenly by Russian nationalists).

Such negative developments would require NATO and its members to review the planned declines in their defence efforts and to decide how to react to the inevitable enhanced demands from Central Europeans for security guarantees. It was argued above that the position in early 1994 meant that bringing new members into NATO would weaken rather than strengthen European security but a transformed, expansionist Russia would mean that membership issues would have to be re-examined. NATO would have to choose which, if any, new members to take on board and on what terms. There would be no gain for NATO in spelling out in advance how it would behave in the light of specific contingencies but some basic points are apparent.

The first is that incorporating any new members into NATO would raise issues of doctrine, force structure and equipment. In particular, would Western countries find it more acceptable to expand the area of their security guarantees on the basis of a doctrine near to massive retaliation, whereby even in a conventional war there would be a threat to initiate the use of nuclear weapons at an early stage because of the conventional force weaknesses of the newly guaranteed states? Or would the West opt for a doctrine of virtual 'no first use', under which it would plan to defend vigorously all guaranteed territory but signal that such defence would be restricted to conventional forces in the event of a purely conventional attack? A 'no first use' policy would make it easier for NATO to take on new members, and arguably would be a sensible change anyway, if only for its non-proliferation implications noted above.

But new members for NATO would raise issues relating to force structure and equipment in the area of conventional forces as well. Would it be possible to deploy Western forces 'forward' in Central Europe to give NATO's new obligations real credibility without giving the Russians a chance to claim that the CFE Treaty had been violated? NATO traditionally used foreign force deployments, especially in Germany, to stress the Alliance's readiness and determination to resist. If regular NATO exercises were to be held in any new member states as a substitute for forward force deployment, such exercises would have to be sufficiently small-scale and infrequent to meet the constraints of agreements made in the CSCE framework. Alternatively, in the light of a serious deterioration in Russian-Western relations, could the West assume that both the CFE Treaty and associated confidence-building measures would collapse?

Clearly one (but only one) of the functions of the Partnership for Peace initiative which NATO launched in January 1994 will be to build appropriate foundations so that new states can be brought smoothly into NATO should the circumstances make it appropriate. The distinguishing characteristic of PFP is that, while the basic agreement between NATO and the partner state has a standard form, the precise list of cooperative activities planned and undertaken under PFP can and will vary from country to country. Partner states including Russia will seek to influence what develops between NATO and other partners but in principle, and to a large degree in practice, NATO should be able to plan customized developments with former Warsaw Pact states in such areas as standardization, air defence integration, operational concepts and procedures, and command, control and identification – all of which would ease the way for new states to become effective new NATO members. However, as PFP develops, NATO will face sensitive choices about which classified information and technology it will release to which partner states. There could be significant differences between NATO members on these issues: the CDU-Liberal government in Germany is seemingly keenest on the rapid security integration of the Central European countries while others such as the US have traditionally been very wary about the transfer of classified information.

Another likely problem in the PFP is that partner countries seeing others developing an intimate relationship on sensitive topics will demand the same treatment for themselves. Currently it is widely thought in NATO that the agenda of cooperation which Russia will build will be rather different from what will be constructed with the Visegrad countries. However, Russia will probably seek to disrupt any such tendency towards a special agenda unless its equal treatment with, for example, Poland would demand an unacceptable degree of transparency about its own defence. However, other countries which would like equal treatment with the Visegrad states, such as the Baltic states and even Ukraine, might have few inhibitions.

These are predictably difficult issues which will require sensitive handling over a protracted period. They are not susceptible to a rapid solution by any formula but awareness of them should make their prudent management easier. A capacity to draw a veil of secrecy over some aspects of PFP activities might be tempting, although advocates of such a course should be ready with answers to the controversy which might follow from the eventual revelation of such secret activities.

Preparing for a hostile Russia would therefore present some difficult issues for NATO but the other, more appealing eventuality is that Russia continues to move towards democracy and a market economy, and accepts as formal equals the states of its former empire. The challenge for NATO then will be to promote the coordinated run-down and reorientation of national defence capabilities among its members.

In the early 1990s NATO's influence on members' policies seemed to be weakening, as member states cut their defence spending unilaterally and in an uncoordinated way. They were motivated first by a diminished sense of threat but more importantly by the impact of economic recession in the West on government tax revenues. There was a particular problem in Germany, which faced the unexpectedly high costs of unification but, across NATO, governments were receiving less revenue than they had anticipated and defence was expected to take its share of the cuts. As a consequence, NATO looked increasingly unlikely to be able to generate the force structures which it had planned in 1991 and was searching for alternative means to coordinate Western capability. While there would be more reaction forces than envisaged – perhaps 10 divisions when only four were thought likely to be needed at any one time – main defence and augmentation units would be fewer than planned, in part because the US looked likely to keep only 75–100,000 troops in Europe rather than the 150,000 of which President Bush had spoken.

NATO's force planning operations clearly need to be reconsidered and revitalized. In the late 1970s, when the perceived need for conventional forces to take a larger share of the burden of deterrence was increasing, NATO states adopted a commitment to increase their real defence spending by three per cent per year. Although flawed in many ways, the three per cent exercise at least provided a framework for a regular collective debate among allies about their changing efforts. Some parallel multilateral guidance should be considered to direct the current downward movements in defence spending. Overall, NATO's defence (Article 5) agenda is far from short.

Where nuclear questions, including proliferation concerns, are involved NATO will be less a framework for reaching common decisions and more a forum in which non-nuclear states can seek to lobby those with nuclear weapons. A hostile or a benign or a continuingly uncertain Russia will still present strategic questions for the West. How many and what kind of nuclear weapons does the West need, and by what doctrine should nuclear forces be guided? In particular, if existing agreements including START 2 are smoothly implemented, there will perhaps be certain questions involving Moscow as a partner as well as a potential adversary, only some of which were noted above in an arms control context. Likely issues include: how are the nuclear states to approach the 1995 review of the NPT? What will be the justification for short- or medium-range air-launched nuclear weapons as START 2 is implemented? Should a comprehensive test ban be agreed? How small would a true minimum deterrent be? What should be the place of ballistic missile defences in Western security, and how much cooperation should there be with Russia on their development and deployment? As indicated earlier, many of these relate to the fundamental issue of whether the existing nuclear states should adopt a long-term goal of removing nuclear weapons as a factor in world politics overall, as some key states such as Japan and perhaps Germany would prefer.

On such matters, NATO's role seems likely to be limited to being a forum for European and Canadian communication with the United States, which inevitably has the lead role. Within Europe, Britain and France are best placed to exercise influence because of their nuclear capabilities and expertise but they will find it hard to have a major impact or even to go their own way when the US and Russia find themselves in a clear accord. Thus Britain and France would find it difficult to carry on testing if the US and Russia finally choose to stop,[2] to stay out of disarmament negotiations after implementation of START 2 or to veto US ballistic missile defence cooperation with Russia.

The role of NATO on nuclear matters will be similar in future to what it has been in the past. National debates and decisions will dominate, with the United States having by far the heaviest impact of the three nuclear powers in NATO. But NATO will be the focal body for Western governments which are seeking to influence nuclear thinking and to evolve common stances on weapons and doctrinal issues. Unless NATO can serve as an effective forum to encourage full discussion and thorough debate, and to enhance the sensitivity of NATO members to each other's concerns, important divisions among allies could appear. On the grounds that reducing nuclear forces requires as much careful thought as their build-up, there are grounds for saying that the Nuclear Planning Group ought to be reinvigorated and that Alliance nuclear matters should not be excluded from the areas in which West Europeans, through the WEU, seek to form an effective caucus within NATO.

When attention is turned to the five other goals for Western policy (preventing the proliferation of weapons of mass destruction, furthering cooperative relations in the former Soviet empire, making the UN Security Council work effectively, building economic growth and promoting democracy in the FSU), it must be recognized that NATO cannot easily take the lead, but could often contribute.

Countering proliferation

On proliferation, the FSU raises many issues: NATO has more relevance in some than others. In the immediate short term, the states best equipped to help with the safe storage, transport and dismantling of nuclear weapons are the Western nuclear powers. Yet they need to coordinate their efforts and may also appreciate help from other NATO members in some fields, including the provision of intelligence about the latest situation in the FSU. NATO meetings may be able to play a coordinating role in some matters.

The ending of Ukrainian nuclear ambitions in particular will require a sustained, clear and coherent Western response in which national actions will be important, in particular the provision of positive and negative security assurances for non-nuclear countries by the established nuclear states, and the linking of economic and other relations to nuclear disarmament and non-proliferation. In the summer of 1993 there had been worrying signs that Germany was being drawn into giving economic support to Ukraine,[3] despite its ambivalent nuclear stance, although the EC Copenhagen summit sensibly sent a clear signal that close relations with Ukraine would not be established until the nuclear position had improved.[4]

The export of both technology and people from the FSU needs to be controlled for non-proliferation purposes. Here there is a place for bilateral cooperation on how to establish and operate paper controls including licences as well as customs machinery. Western expertise is located primarily in states rather than in international bodies. Institutionally the main Western coordinating body until March 1994 was Cocom, which after the end of the Cold War acquired a slightly more transparent character than before.

Cocom's evolution towards a more positive cooperation with former communist states had taken a major turn in June 1992 when it decided to invite such states to form a Cocom Cooperation Forum on Export Controls, rather in parallel with the NACC. The Forum, which met for the first time in November 1992, was meant to coordinate Western help to the former communist states on the establishment of new export control regimes and to agree procedures, including perhaps on-site inspections, to prevent the diversion of Western technology supplied to the East for unauthorized purposes. As noted above, the NACC agreed in November the terms which would protect the abuse of Western technology supplied to the former communist bloc.

Cocom planned a three-stage process for the easing of export control. Once a state had an export control system in place and had agreed not to divert technology to military uses, it was entitled to 'favourable consideration' for its technology requests. Poland, the Czech Republic, Slovakia, Romania and Bulgaria achieved this status by the spring of 1993. Once export controls had been seen to be working, countries could move to a second stage of 'administrative exception', whereby Cocom states merely inform their partners of any Cocom-listed items they export. The final stage was complete removal from Cocom procedures.

However, by late 1993, although Russia was seeking to buy only a few of the very sophisticated items still left on the Cocom Industrial List, it protested firmly against the restrictions on it as a democratic state and Cocom's members lost determination to maintain controls. In November

1993 they agreed to wind up Cocom by the end of March 1994 and to put a new organization including Russia in its place. Details of the new organization's role had not been fixed by June,[5] although the US was keen that it should concentrate on targeting states of particular concern such as North Korea and Iran.

The likely creation of an export control body which includes Russia and Ukraine has implications for NATO. The new body needs to coordinate help to FSU successor states so that they can establish effective technology export controls. It needs to monitor technology flowing to the developing world so that surreptitious proliferation efforts can be identified and prevented. It also needs to stimulate intellectual exchanges among the technological experts of participating countries to ensure that lists of products which need to be controlled are up-to-date. However, this leaves a role for NATO as a private forum for Western discussions on technology transfer issues and on technology flows to the FSU. This is broadly compatible with NATO's new explicit concern with proliferation.

The North Atlantic Council should be a vital forum advancing the coordination of Western policy on proliferation, since North American and West European states are accustomed to meeting there regularly at a high level for the discussion of security issues. Western cohesion needs to be sustained, for instance on what types of Russian arms exports are reasonable, and on what sorts of pressure should be exerted on Russia not to export dual-use components for the Indian space launcher programme. All the regimes inhibiting the proliferation of weapons of mass destruction and ballistic missiles have their separate consultation forums, but the Council is uniquely able to work towards a coherent Western view.

Building cooperative relations

As regards building cooperative relations within the former Soviet empire, the CSCE process rather than NATO provides a foundation for Western efforts. Through the CSCE, norms of interstate relations for Europe have been articulated and agreed, and a modest machinery has been set up to make these norms respected in practice, most recently in the Helsinki Declaration. CSCE commitments are a central element in the Russian-US security assurances envisaged for Ukraine. Crucially, by including all the successor states in the CSCE framework when the USSR broke up, the West signalled that all parts of the FSU were expected to respect the CSCE regime. Perhaps the biggest conceptual and practical challenge remaining for CSCE will be to reinforce provision for the protection of minority rights within a state, possibly using principles similar to those outlined in Chapter 5, since the perceived abuse of such rights, in Russia and many other successor states, has the potential to stimulate both internal and cross-border strife. The appointment of a CSCE Commissioner on National Minorities after the CSCE Helsinki meeting was a helpful first step, but no more than that, in the development of international institutional capability to act in this area. The CSCE in 1993 and 1994, through words of caution to Estonia and Latvia preceded by investigation and monitoring, helped to reduce friction in the region.[6] However, despite the best efforts of the CSCE representatives, force still plays a big role in the Nagorny Karabakh, Trans-Dnestr, Tajikistan and Georgian conflicts.

A significant advance would be to build minority rights protection into the legal commitments made by Council of Europe members under the European Convention on Human Rights. This would enable legally backed investigations to be made into alleged abuses and could strengthen implementation of standards first agreed in the CSCE. The first meeting of the Council of Europe at Heads of Government level in October 1993 sadly did not make much progress in this area.[7]

Although the CSCE is the leading body in the minority rights area, NATO can make a continuing triple contribution in promoting cooperative relations as a whole. First, it can serve as a forum in which coherent Western positions are developed. While France in particular has always been concerned about the prominence of NATO in pan-European debates, because it was associated with American dominance, it must be recognized that, if France and Germany argue one line in the CSCE and the US asserts another, the result will simply be Western ineffectiveness. The CSCE has also been targeted as an area in which common European Union policies should be formulated,[8] suggesting the need for a dual process of coordination (intra-EU and EU–NATO).

A second contribution is that NATO's very existence can discourage improper behaviour. Any Russian government, no matter how inclined towards the control of its neighbours, knows that, so long as NATO exists, any serious act of aggression against its neighbours would bring coherent and effective sanctions at a time when Russia needs Western technology (and food). NATO's membership might also be widened. Russia also knows that any power gains it made would be marginal and that it would never be allowed to dominate all Europe. Also, even if no NATO member were attacked, Russia could not be sure that in the event military help might not be forthcoming for the attacked state.

A third role for NATO will be to steer the future development of pan-European conventional arms control which will be based in a CSCE framework through the Vienna Forum for Security Cooperation. As argued above, unless the Russian polity changes suddenly for the worse, thus wrecking arms control prospects, the main role for conventional arms control in the next decade should be to help shape cooperative relations in the East.

NATO is the obvious body to coordinate Western direction of the broad shape of negotiations, although arms control is a field where the quality of a proposal counts, not its birthplace, and there is a place for initiatives from both national governments and European bodies including the WEU. Rapid progress towards agreements need not be expected or even sought. What will count is that countries, through discussions, learn about one another's concerns and fears, and, as new states, get into a habit of looking for confidence-building measures and arms control. Without outside help, the new states of the FSU will make little progress in this area: the heritage of former communist control provides them with little readiness for such progress.

More scepticism should be voiced about the value of Western peacekeeping forces for CSCE areas with NATO labels attached. NATO decided in 1992 that it could provide such forces for both CSCE and UN operations.[9] In practice, as experience with Bosnia has shown, any such operations may stimulate nationalist fears in Russia about NATO's growing aspirations and will make it harder to involve FSU forces in peacekeeping operations with the West. More prudent steps would be to sustain NATO as an organization which, through its planning, exercises and consultations, enables Western forces to work together in many types of operation and which is on occasion ready to see even its own resources (such as infrastructure elements and the AWACs fleet) released for other purposes when a NATO label was not involved.

Peacekeeping operations, broadly defined, are more likely to have political appeal if they have a NACC label from the beginning, rather than a NATO designation. There are important efforts under way to cooperate in the NACC on peacekeeping, by working together on concepts, procedures, troop training, logistics, communications and command, through the NACC Ad Hoc Group on Peacekeeping.[10] Such efforts both provide opportunities for the armed forces of the FSU and the West to make personal contact and enhance the chance that any peacekeeping operations mounted will be professionally and effectively executed. The Russian political spectrum would find it easiest initially to welcome peacekeepers from the European NNA states on missions in the FSU itself. Thus initiatives involving Sweden in peacekeeping preparation and cooperation, such as at the NACC High Level Seminar on Peacekeeping at the end of June 1993, should be welcomed, and Switzerland's decision to avoid participation in peacekeeping activities is to be regretted.

In January 1994 NATO formally launched its PFP initiative which, as noted, could serve to enhance the NACC as a means of building cooperation with former adversaries and prepare some states politically and militarily to enter the alliance. The kinds of activity which the PFP initiative could promote have been discussed above. Perhaps the most telling institutional points are, first, that NATO staff will not find it easy to coordinate or even keep track of the many bilateral security links developing between NATO members and former Warsaw Pact states; and, second, that PFP and the NACC have a limited future if NATO states do not commit significant resources to their activities. The sums involved need to be in the region of hundreds, rather than tens, of millions of dollars.

The long-term outlook for cooperative Russian-Western relations beyond the military sector is certain to be marked by suspicion and periodic hostility, unless Moscow and St Petersburg can be made to be feel truly European cities, and unless Russia west of the Urals sees itself as part of Europe. As Presidents Havel and Walesa recognized when they first visited NATO, Russia must be integrated into Europe over the long term. The main responsibility for creating the economic and social ties which will influence the wider attitudes of many Russians will be carried by the EU. There is thus a clear danger that an implicit division of labour, with the EU and WEU concentrating on Hungary, Poland, the Czech Republic, Slovakia, Bulgaria, Romania, and even the Baltic states while the US dominates Western relations with Russia, could reinforce rather than weaken Russia's sense of separation from Europe as a whole. While Moscow may be drawn to a special relationship with Washington which hints at equality of status between the two nuclear superpowers, and while the WEU may want to opt for a narrower range of dialogue partners in the East than NATO, to prevent charges of duplication, the long-term foundation for cooperation between Russia and Europe can only be a multitude of economic, social and cultural ties as well as security links.

The United Nations, the CSCE and global order

The capacity of the CSCE to substitute for the UN is limited, since four of the five permanent members of the UNSC can also paralyse the CSCE. However, the UN may prefer to see some missions based in the CSCE rather than in the UN itself, thereby relieving the overloaded

UN staff of a supervisory burden. Yet institutionally the CSCE is not well equipped to supervise tricky peacekeeping operations which encounter the kind of day-to-day dilemmas experienced by the UN forces in the former Yugoslavia and Somalia. Moreover, as argued earlier, Russia is more likely to value the UN if the UN itself shows a concern with and a readiness to commit resources to the territories by which Russia feels most threatened, which are basically in the successor states of the FSU. With regard to peacekeeping in the FSU, the traditional UN practice that neighbouring states or the previously imperial state should not provide forces is simply not practical. Nor, apparently, is the traditional UN rule that peacekeeping must always have the consent of the parties:[11] in former Yugoslavia the UN-sanctioned blockade of Serbia and the Bosnia no-fly zone are scarcely supported by the Serbs.

On the institutional dimension of peacekeeping in the FSU, the West needs to recognize fundamental realities, to keep a firm eye on a realistic and valued target, and to work for long-term change. Important fundamental realities for the moment are that outside states are not sufficiently concerned with the FSU to provide the forces needed there to restrict and manage conflicts, and that Russia will not accept that it needs a mandate for intervention from states which are unwilling to contribute either troops or money. A realistic and valued target for the West is that security in the FSU should not become acknowledged as solely Russia's responsibility, and that it should be organized as much as possible in a multilateral framework. The UN and more immediately the CSCE are the most relevant frameworks, and the West should continue to work for these bodies to play peacemaking and observation roles whenever possible. Russia has allowed several such missions to date and CSCE representatives have also been accepted by the parties directly involved in conflicts. Although it has not yet proved possible for the CSCE to generate draft rules acceptable to Russia to cover peacekeeping in the FSU,[12] attempts should continue in this area and to get Russia to appreciate the value of an international mandate. In the longer term, outside states may be persuaded to make either a financial or a military contribution (or both) to peacekeeping in the FSU, as a means of encouraging Russia to renounce any aspirations to act on a unilateral basis.

There are three other fundamental institutional points regarding the UN. First, insofar as Russia may need to be rewarded for its cooperation in the UNSC, the money and favours will have to be forthcoming from the West through the EBRD, the IMF and the G7 as well as the EU and national governments which can grant market access to Russian goods as well as providing aid.

Second, as noted, the NACC and PFP preparations in peacekeeping cooperation should enhance the quality of UN forces overall. There is no reason why NACC-prepared forces should be limited to missions in the CSCE area.

Third, possible reform of the UN, in particular the modification of permanent Security Council membership to include Japan, Germany, Brazil and India, will not only make Britain and France feel nervous about their status: Moscow too will be affected and should be closely consulted by the West during the possibly drawn-out reform process so that it does not feel isolated.

Economic growth

Over the longer term, the readiness of former Soviet nuclear, chemical and biological weapons scientists to deny their services to potential employers beyond Russia will depend on their economic opportunities at home. Economic advance or its absence will indeed influence many aspects of relations within the FSU and between FSU states and their external neighbours. Such opportunities will reflect both the readiness of FSU governments to institute economic reform and the West's capacity and readiness to support such reform with technical aid and investment programmes. These are matters initially for the IMF, the EBRD and for national capitals, although the EU will seek to coordinate and enhance the performance of its members, and the G7 could develop a particular role with regard to integrating help to the

FSU on a global scale. Without pressure exercised through the G7, and given that the dispute about the Northern Territories is so far from resolution, it is hard to see how Japan will be induced to deepen its commitment to strengthening the Russian economy.

As noted, economic development involves the issue of conversion, of transferring effectively many of the human and material resources used in the military sector to the civil. NATO has moved tentatively in this area, presenting it as part of the NACC agenda and holding a major conference, with the NATO Economics Directorate having the lead role. Unlike the EU, NATO has little experience with industrial adjustment matters. Yet that may not matter too much. The fundamental problems with conversion are not institutional. They stem from the facts, put simply, that no one knows how to do it, and in Russia and Ukraine many of the military are anyway wary for strategic reasons of abandoning defence industrial capabilities. The West in the early 1990s is marked by recession and a decline in manufacturing, and resources freed by lower defence spending are not being used for other purposes. If Western governments cannot stimulate the much smaller-scale conversion of either factories or regions in their own economies, there is little chance that they will be able to do much in any organizational framework for the successor republics to the Soviet Union.[13] On the defence conversion issue, NATO is not particularly well qualified to produce initiatives, but in the absence of credible alternatives, it can do little harm to see what contribution it can make and in 1993 it was concentrating on the generation of databases of defence conversion expertise and military industrial plants needing conversion.[14] Pilot projects were also under study.

On the other hand, even in the short term, Russians and Ukrainians will judge what they should do about their own defence industrial bases and set the reconstitution demands which they want to build into it, partly by reference to what the West does about its own defence industry in Europe and the US. A NACC dialogue on the strategic aspects of defence industries is not immediately necessary, but it is an issue in which Moscow has traditionally been interested and remains so:

Russia is preparing a new law on mobilization preparation in the Russian Federation.[15] The continued state control of major manufacturing concerns which could well be involved could hinder privatization. A future confidence-building task will be to ensure that neither Russia nor the West feels it would lose a defence industrial mobilization race in the event of political relations threatening to deteriorate.

Democracy and control of the military

In international organizational terms, the building of liberal, democratic political cultures and systems in the FSU is primarily CSCE business, with CSCE agreements setting goals and norms, and national and multilateral programmes playing a big role in their pursuit.

As far as the civilian and democratic control of defence is concerned, the focus for such programmes is and should be the PFP activities and the NACC which already brings together Chiefs of Staff of partner states,[16] holds annual meetings of defence and foreign ministers, and welcomes representatives of partner countries to NATO's political, economic and other committees. It also organizes specialist seminars, helps with military exchanges and enables East European officers to attend training courses in the West.

Like cooperation in peacekeeping, these activities should clearly reassure Eastern military forces about NATO as armed forces become familiar with each other. Western policies on arms control, the withdrawal of Russian forces from the Baltics and even a settlement of the Northern Territories dispute with Japan would have better prospects of success if they enjoyed acceptance by the Russian military.[17] But the NACC should also give more prominence than its current Work Plan indicates to demonstrating how defence can be democratically controlled by civilian authorities. Particularly as far as Russia and Ukraine are concerned, it is important to show how a strong defence is not incompatible with civilian authority. This entails educating FSU military personnel about the operation of Western systems (which are quite varied) and also training civilians in a number of areas: the ways in which parliamentary defence committees can be made to work; the role of publicly available information about defence in a democracy; methods of budgeting and financial control, procurement and contracting techniques, and project management, including collaborative project management. In such matters the UK experience should have particular relevance for FSU forces since, despite their civilian masters, the effectiveness of the UK armed forces is widely recognized. In Russia a crucial first stage will be for the military to be taken out of politics in accordance with the 1993 military doctrine and for the legislature to gain experience in the approval of real defence spending, for from control of the money can flow many other elements of civilian control over defence. This in turn rests on the premise that more or less all defence spending is included in the defence budget and the NACC, by promoting dialogue on the common definition of defence spending which the UN has long pursued, could make a real contribution to parliamentary power in many states. As signalled earlier, effective civilian and parliamentary supervision of defence in Russia needs to be seen as a long-term task: in 1994 many in the Russian parliament seemed more keen to use the defence budget to make difficulties for President Yeltsin than to treat defence responsibly. Those running the NACC and the PFP therefore need to be ready for a long-term programme to enforce awareness of such matters as the advantages for the military of enjoying public and parliamentary support, and the gains for politicians of having at their disposal military forces which are cost-effective and broadly defined, which respect political direction, and which the country can afford over the long term. It is encouraging to note that, while Russian serving officers were allowed to stand for election to the parliament under the 1993 Russian constitution, it seems that the half-dozen or so who were elected will go into the reserve for their terms as parliamentarians.

To change views held about the West in the FSU must be recognized as a long-term process which will take a decade or more. The NACC, like other Western organizations, must prepare itself for a sustained effort where rapid results cannot be expected. But NATO should move quickly to provide the NACC with more resources and to sort out internal problems with the NACC's operation. In particular the roles of the NATO Military Committee, the Military Cooperation Programme, and the Group on Defence Matters, need to be harmonized.[18] The NACC process must also make sure its long-term aims of building military contacts and cooperation on peacekeeping are not overshadowed at senior political meetings by discussions of particular conflicts more appropriately discussed in a CSCE context.

Conclusion

In building on this complex, multi-dimensional picture, some points merit particular emphasis.

First, many international bodies will make a contribution to the West's changing security relationship with Russia. They will have overlapping concerns, with different organizations taking the lead depending on the issue. This means that they will have to find new ways of cooperating among themselves, as well as of making their member states coordinate their activities. A reasonable start has been made with the recent closer EU and WEU contacts with NATO, but much remains to be done. As students of international organizations are aware, there is a vast literature in international relations on how states cooperate. However, comparatively little is known about ways of promoting effective cooperation among international organizations, in part because cooperation among them is quite rare.

As argued, NATO should not have the lead in several areas but can often make a specific contribution: it can serve as the obvious forum where West European and North American views can be quietly and informally coordinated on many topics. This suggests that NATO could well have a future as a background organization: the place where common Western policies can emerge through hidden processes. In the Asia-Pacific region, one of Japan's perceived economic strengths has been its capacity to coordinate when necessary the activities of its government, finance sector and major industrial groups through discreet networks. NATO, in so far as it coordinated the West in the past, tended to proclaim its achievements in public. In future, it may usefully become a little more opaque in its operations, like the cooperative frameworks which are so effective in Japan.

Second, it must be stressed that the West in principle has three limited assets which it must use well — brainpower, solidarity, and wealth. Its military power will provide a defence against the FSU states (especially Russia) if necessary but will be of little use in transforming its political relationship with the successor states, except that the West may on occasion be able to provide peacekeeping/police forces to troubled areas through the NACC and in collaboration with Eastern partners. However in 1994 the West's intellectual, economic and even military assets looked more than a little flawed:

- it seemingly lacked the intellectual and policy tools to be confident about ending recession and instituting sustained economic growth;
- the demands for aid and investment on the West's wealth from East/Central Europe, the FSU, North Africa and the wider world greatly exceeded any funds which it could provide; and
- Western solidarity was breaking up over trade disputes and uncoordinated, unilateral national moves to cut defence spending.

These Western weaknesses therefore should be targeted by governments as urgent areas for repair.

Third, the end of the Cold War means the start of a long journey for the West. A satisfactory new relationship with successor states of the FSU cannot be defined overnight, not least because of the uncertainty which marks Russia and many other republics. NATO members must see the PFP agreements, the NACC and the CSCE, for instance, as needing a decade or so to make significant progress in all aspects of their work. Appropriate new economic and social ties within the East, and between East and West in Europe, will take many years to build up, especially if Western Europe continues to be reluctant to open its markets to cheap goods from the East.

On this long journey, NATO has few financial resources to promote change in the FSU but the NACC surely merits more than the $10 million or so which it spent in 1992, given the importance of its tasks. Significantly, the need of Eastern delegations to pay their own fares to NACC meetings was one reason why many of the poorer FSU states were absent from many NACC gatherings. Consideration of what might reasonably be spent on NACC, and on PFP, and indeed on all efforts to promote cooperative relations and prevent the reversion of Moscow to an intimidatory stance should bear in mind the peace dividend which the West has already enjoyed, largely without noticing it because of the much larger negative effects of economic recession. Clearly it is impossible to say incontrovertibly what would have been spent on defence had the Cold War continued, but it is reasonable to assume that a hostile Soviet Union would have led the West to spend a constant share of GDP on defence. Between 1980 and 1984, defence spending in NATO Europe averaged 3.6 per cent of GDP; in 1992 it was estimated to have fallen to 2.7 per cent. For North America the comparable figures were 5.5 and 5.1 per cent, although between 1985 and 1989 defence's share of GDP actually rose to 6 per cent. For NATO Europe, the peace dividend appears to be roughly around one per cent of GDP so far, which in the case of the UK is around $15 billion. Spending on the NACC and PFP should be evaluated in the light of what these bodies can continue to contribute to more cooperative security relations (and so lower Western defence spending).

For many, the analysis here will suggest a pessimistic conclusion, that the West will be unable to take advantage of the end of the Cold War to build a new set of pan-European relationships which involve integrating Russia into the wider Europe. Western governments, some would assert, are incapable of the long-term, coordinated action, and international organizations are clearly incapable of working together effectively. This leads to a counsel of despair, that Russia should be written off and the West should be content with defending against it as far east as is practicable. Some would argue the merits of the eastern German border, others the value of the Polish border, while others would assert the significance and potential of Ukraine.

But this thinking should be rejected as at least premature. There are no preordained limits to the West's ability to devise new modes of cooperation for long-term purposes. There are today in the CSCE area many forms of cooperation which would have been unthinkable 30 years ago and yet more evolution in cooperation must be attempted. The West must seek to move closer to Russia, to seize the 'neo-idealist moment', while keeping NATO as a non-provocative insurance policy in case things go wrong. This will undoubtedly involve the prudent granting to Russia of great-power status, and of Western recognition that Russia is the most important variable in the future security of Eastern Europe. Handling this will not be easy. For instance, Russia was properly not given a special status under the PFP programme and was offered the same standard agreement as other states. However, a separate agreement assuring Russia's particular importance and potential was also agreed, and Russia will clearly be able to negotiate its own individual list of cooperative activities undertaken in the PFP framework. This offers a chance to treat it in a special way. Measures which cost little but have important psychological effects, such as US Secretary of State Warren Christopher telling his opposite number Andrei Kozyrev that 'I may be senior in chronology, but we're full and equal partners in every other respect',[19] have real value, as does NATO's acknowledgment of Russia as a 'major European, world and nuclear power'.[20] Russia should overall be treated as a permanent member of the UNSC, not least because the West wants Russia to behave in accordance with the norms of that organization, and if that means allowing Russia to join the G7, perhaps as the price for Russia signing a PFP agreement, the West should be ready to accept that. Russia's presence would scarcely undermine the political effectiveness of an already unproductive G7 framework and may even strengthen it. In its treatment of Russia, the West should also seek to win endorsement for its policies from other Central and East European states, which should conclude that Western policies in the long term should enhance their security.

The end of the Cold War has forced many policy practitioners as well as academics to reconsider what they see as the fundamental concepts and theories pertinent to international political life. During the Cold War, the emphasis of the former Soviet Union on totalitarian government and the strengths and goals of communism, coupled with the conventional and nuclear military strength deployed by Moscow, meant that those Western analysts who stressed the importance of domestic political systems in shaping foreign policy did not seriously quarrel with those who endorsed the political realist school, which asserted that all states rationally seek to maximize their power, regardless of their political system. Both schools accepted the need to defend and deter with regard to Soviet military capability. The collapse of both the Soviet Union and the communist government in Moscow has brought a need for the reformulation of basic guiding ideas.

In these circumstances, the most useful idea from the broad theoretical tool-box of International Relations as an academic subject vis-à-vis the management by the West of the FSU is arguably that of a 'regime'. This admittedly flexible concept emerged during the 1980s as a shorthand way of explaining how particular areas of international life were provided with order and predictability, and the stress was on the different, mutually reinforcing contributions which could be made, in an area such as trade, by a range of factors including international law, international organizations, norms of behaviour, morality, political power, transnational pressure groups and so on. The West should recognize that the security problems presented by the collapse of the Soviet Union and the subsequent centrality of Russia need to be handled through the development of a regime comprising not one but a range of international organizations (NATO, the EU, the CSCE, the UN and so on). This regime needs to include both legal constraints on behaviour, in such documents as the UN Charter and arms control treaties, and norms of behaviour which may either be explicitly articulated in documents such as the Paris Charter, or remain implicit. A Western consensus on the implicit dimension of the regime, and in particular about the limits of acceptable Russian behaviour in the CIS, will not be easy to forge. In this regime there must be a role both for Western power to deter and defend, and for extensive Western cooperation with and integration of the societies of the FSU. The West needs to be both realist, i.e. sensitive to power, and idealist, i.e. not placing limits on the potential of cooperation. The notion of a regime also serves as a reminder that the security issues emanating from the FSU are not short-term. More often, as is apparent from the analysis above, they are long-term, not susceptible to a quick solution, and in need of monitoring, control, containment and management. With all its limitations, the idea of a regime best encapsulates the desired characteristics of Western policy.

Neither scholars nor political practitioners well understand what causes the threat and use of force to become unthinkable in the relations among specific states, so establishing pluralistic security communities. However, it would seem likely that cultural, scientific, social, economic and political links all have a place.[21] The appeal of such communities should not be underestimated. From the perspective of societies in the former Soviet empire, the establishment and durability of the North Atlantic security community must seem a remarkable and valuable achievement. Such thinking indicates that cultural and other links, involving Russian participation in everything from European sporting contests, piano competitions and the Eurovision song contest to inter-town exchanges, art exhibitions and pop concerts, can make a long-term contribution to international security. The Council of Europe could have a real impact on relations with Russia, once Moscow can claim to be ready and qualified to join. But over time cultural ties need to be supplemented by economic and many other links among peoples and governments, which makes the EU particularly relevant.

This is not to assert that Russia should become a member of the EU, but it is to argue that eventually Russia must have good market access to the Union, that trade between the two should be substantial, that there should be significant cross-investment, mutual recognition of professional qualifications and technical standards, and that Russia should have a voice as EU technical standards and regulations are being developed. In 40 years time, the Russia-EU relationship must be a close one if broadly cooperative political relations are to be reliably in place. In the long term, Russia will either have to be defended against by the West, or become part of the North Atlantic security community.

NOTES

Chapter 1: Introduction

1 John Lewis Gaddis, 'International Relations Theory and the End of the Cold War', *International Security*, vol. 17, no. 3, winter 1992–3, p. 5.

2 See for instance Richard Ullman, 'Redefining Security', *International Security*, vol. 8, no. 1, summer 1983, pp. 129–54; Jessica Tuchman Mathews, 'Redefining Security', *Foreign Affairs*, vol. 68, no. 2, spring 1989, pp. 162–78; Barry Buzan, 'New World Realpolitik: New patterns of global security in the twenty-first century', *International Affairs*, vol. 67, no. 3, July 1991, p. 433; Barry Buzan, *People, States and Fear: an agenda for international security studies in the post-Cold War era*, Hemel Hempstead, Harvester-Wheatsheaf, 1991; Ken Booth, 'Security and Emancipation', *Review of International Studies*, vol. 17, no. 4, October 1991, p. 319; Teresa Pelton Johnson, 'Writing for *International Security*: A Contributor's Guide', *International Security*, vol. 16, no. 2, fall 1991, p. 172. For a recent analysis of the relationship of environmental developments to the threat and use of force, see Thomas F. Homer-Dixon, 'On the Threshold: Environmental Changes as Causes of Acute Conflict', *International Security*, vol. 16, no. 2, fall 1991, pp. 76–116. On migration as a source of dispute and conflict among states, see Myron Wiener, 'Security, Stability and International Migration', *International Security*, vol. 17, no. 3, winter 1992–3, pp. 91–126.

As a reminder of how a broad definition of security can lead to a state claiming the right to monitor large areas of its citizens' lives, A. Hasnan Habib wrote that 'for Indonesia security ... includes all aspects of national life: ideological, political, economic, social, cultural and military. Indonesia's concept of security is, therefore, complex and multi-dimensional', in 'Indonesia's Defence Industry: Its role, mission and set-up' in Chanduran Jeshuran (ed.), *Arms and Defence in Southeast Asia*, Singapore, Institute for South-East Asian Studies, 1989, p. 70. As Ullman acknowledges, there is often a trade-off between liberty and security, *op. cit.*, pp. 130–31.

3 These have been explored in a series of volumes emerging from a joint project linking the Royal Institute of International Affairs in London and the Institute for International Policy Studies in Tokyo. See T. Taylor (ed.), *The Collapse of the Soviet Empire*, London, RIIA, 1992; S. Sato and T. Taylor (eds), *Prospects for Global Order*, London, RIIA, 1993; R. Imai and T. Taylor (eds), *The Defence*

Trade, London, RIIA, 1994; and T. Taylor and S. Sato (eds), *Future Sources of Global Conflict* (forthcoming, 1994).

Chapter 2: Proliferation and direct military threats

1 'Poles reach Soviet pull-out deal', *The Financial Times*, 9 October 1991.

2 Taras Kuzio, *Ukraine: the Unfinished Revolution*, London, Institute for European Defence and Strategic Studies (European Security Study No. 16), p. 36.

3 Quoted from Mary C. Fitzgerald, 'Russia's New Military Doctrine', *RUSI Journal*, vol. 137, no. 5, October 1992, p. 45. This paragraph and those following draw heavily on the material collected in the Fitzgerald article, as well as from C. J. Dick, *Counter-Blows in Russian Military Thinking*, Sandhurst, Soviet Studies Research Centre (SSRC), Royal Military Academy (RMA), December 1992, especially para. 37.

4 Mikhail V. Berdennikov, 'Russia's New Military Doctrine', *RUSI Journal*, vol. 137, no. 6, December 1992, p. 7. Berdennikov is a Russian Foreign Ministry official. See also James F. Holcomb, *Russian Military Doctrine*, Sandhurst, SSRC, RMA, August 1992, p. 2.

5 See the material collected by P. H. Vigor and M. J. Orr, *Future Russian Security Policies – A Military-Scientific Conference*, Sandhurst, SSRC, RMA, November 1992, pp. 4–8.

6 'A major problem of strategic deployment, and particularly of transition from peacetime to wartime, is that the most heavily populated part of Russia, i.e. the European part, falls within the purview of the Paris Treaty. Equipment can be stored in Siberia but how are personnel drawn from the central parts of Russia to be married up with equipment reserves beyond the Urals?', quoted by Vigor and Orr, *op. cit.*, p. 12. See also Pavel S. Grachev, 'Drafting a New Russian Military Doctrine', *Military Technology*, vol. 17, no. 2, pp. 10–17.

7 James Sherr, *Living with Russia in the Post-Soviet Era*, Sandhurst, SSRC, RMA, July 1992, pp. 4–6. He notes the unresolved dilemmas of Russia with regard to the KGB, whose files on internal security remain largely closed: 'either the Russian Federation bases its legitimacy on revolution against the USSR, in which case the KGB becomes as much an enemy of the Russian government as the STB became of Vaclav Havel's government; or it bases its authority on continuity with the USSR, in which case it undermines its own demand for a transformed relationship with the West' (p. 3).

8 Pavel S. Grachev in *Military Technology*, *op. cit.*, p. 10.

9 J.B.K. Lough, *The Russian Army Enters Politics*, Sandhurst, SSRC, RMA, July 1992, p. 4.

10 See C.J. Dick, 'Initial Thoughts on Russia's Draft Military Doctrine', *SSRC Occasional Brief* no. 12, Sandhurst, SSRC, RMA, 14 July 1992.

11 Berdennikov, *op. cit.*, p. 6. See note 4.

12 Dick, *op. cit.*, p. 9.

13 See C.J. Dick, 'Russia's Draft Military Doctrine, 10 Months On', *SSRC*

Occasional Brief no. 17, Sandhurst, SSRC, RMA, April 1993.

14 J.B.K. Lough, 'Redefining Russia's Role in the Near Abroad', Sandhurst, SSRC, RMA, April 1993, p. 10.

15 *Ibid.*

16 *Ibid.*, p. 11.

17 'Yeltsin attacks army chiefs', *Independent*, 27 July 1993.

18 Joint Russian Defence and Foreign Ministry statement, see BBC *SWB* SU/1971 B/5, 14 April 1994.

19 The November doctrine was widely reported in the Western press but for a detailed analysis see C.J. Dick, *The Military Doctrine of the Russian Federation*, Sandhurst, SSRC, RMA, November 1993, from which the quotations are taken.

20 'Visiting Switzerland: Grachev defines "near abroad"', *International Defense Review*, vol. 27, no. 1, January 1994, p. 5.

21 BBC *SWB* SU/1966 B/7, 8 April 1994; BBC *SWB* SU/1967 B/4-5, 9 April 1994.

22 The CIS Command was to be replaced by a CIS military cooperation body which Shaposhnikov's deputy, Col. General Viktor Samsonov, was to chair. See 'CIS Move Stalls Pact on Security', *Defense News*, 21–27 June 1993.

23 *Soviet Nuclear Fission: Control of the Nuclear Arsenal in a Disintegrating Soviet Union*, Cambridge, MA, Centre for Science and International Affairs, Kennedy School of Government, Harvard University, 1991, digested in 'Stuff of Western nightmares', *The Financial Times*, 10 December 1991.

24 BBC *SWB* SU/1958 S1/1, 29 March 1994.

25 Bruce Blair, *The Logic of Accidental Nuclear War*, Washington DC, Brookings Books, April 1993, p. 259.

26 'Disused arms "threaten new Chernobyls"', *Independent*, 5 February 1992.

27 'Ukraine N-arms leaking radiation', *The Financial Times*, 3 March 1993. For the environmental problems faced by Russian nuclear submarines, see a Greenpeace report digested in 'Russian submarines still risk meltdown', *Jane's Defence Weekly*, 6 March 1993, p. 7.

28 The renewal/extension of the treaty will in any case face difficulties through the West's preference to hold at least some nuclear tests and the refusal of existing nuclear powers to commit themselves to giving up their nuclear forces completely.

29 For the confusion associated with the Minsk summit from the beginning, see 'A further step towards separatism', *The Financial Times*, 17 February 1992.

30 'Shaposhnikov gives pledge on missiles', *The Financial Times*, 31 January 1992.

31 Ukraine, like other FSU republics, agreed at the December 1991 Alma Ata meeting to allow the transfer to Russia by 1 July 1992 of all the tactical nuclear weapons on its territory. These were believed to number 2,500; 57 per cent of them had been moved by March when they were stopped on the orders of President Kravchuk. The Ukrainian leader said that the transfer of these weapons would not continue until Moscow agreed to international supervision of their destruction or allowed their destruction in the West. Such supervision,

however, was not a condition of the December agreement; see, *inter alia*, 'CIS ministers fall out over nuclear arms', *The Times*, 2 April 1992.

32 The Supreme Council of the Ukraine on 5 December 1991 issued a statement declaring that 'Ukraine will not be a nuclear power'. However, it also indicated that it saw itself as a party to the START 1 Treaty (so rejecting the view that Russia was the sole successor to the Soviet Union's nuclear disarmament commitments) and that Ukraine saw its non-nuclear status as a matter for international negotiation rather than unilateral action; see 'Open Letter to Parliaments and Peoples of the World', *The Ukrainian Review*, spring 1992, p. 75. This is in contrast to 'the status and future of Crimea, which cannot be the subject of international relations', see Appeal of the Supreme Council of Ukraine to the North Atlantic Assembly, 4 June 1992, in *The Ukrainian Review*, autumn 1992, p. 93.

33 'Kravchuk Urges Nuke Pullout', *Defense News*, 11–17 May 1992.

34 Peter van Ham, *Ukraine, Russia and European Security*, Chaillot Paper no. 13, Paris, WEU Institute for Security Studies, 1994, p. 15.

35 The Belarus parliament ratified START 1 on 4 February and approved the country's signature of the NPT; see 'Pact ratified', *Independent*, 5 February 1993.

36 *The Military Balance: 1992–3*, London, International Institute for Strategic Studies (IISS)/Brassey's, 1992, p. 226.

37 BBC *SWB* SU/1974 S1/4, 18 April 1994; BBC *SWB* SU/1951 S1/4, 21 March 1994.

38 See 'Russia and Ukraine slip towards Slav "cold war"', *The Financial Times*, 30 April 1992.

39 Victor Batiouk, *Ukraine's Non-Nuclear Option*, United Nations Institute for Disarmament Research (UNIDIR), Research Paper no. 14, Geneva, New York, UN, 1992, p. 1.

40 *Ibid.*, p. 7.

41 *Ibid.*, p. 7. Blair (*op. cit.*, p. 261) stresses negative control as the limit of Ukrainian ambitions.

42 Batiouk, *op. cit.*, pp. 12–14. Blair, *op. cit.*, p. 14, says that Yeltsin had agreed not to fire any nuclear weapons without the permission of the Presidents of Ukraine, Belarus and Kazakhstan.

43 See interview with Gen. Leonid Ivashov, Secretary to the CIS Council of Ministers, in *Defense News*, 1–7 March 1993.

44 Ukrainian First Deputy Defence Minister Col. Gen. Ivan Bizha, quoted in 'Deadlock reached on future of CIS forces', *Jane's Defence Weekly*, 30 January 1993.

45 *Ibid.*, p. 5.

46 See, for instance, 'Ex Oriente Lux', *The Ukrainian Review*, spring 1992, pp. 3–12.

47 Vladimir Ruban, 'The Birth of a Military Power', text from Sandhurst, SSRC, RMA, Advab. 827, September 1992.

48 See van Ham, *op. cit.*, for a thorough discussion.

49 Blair, *op. cit.*, p. 258.

50 See, for instance, 'Ukraine divided over N-missiles', *The Financial Times*, 5–6 June 1993.

51 Ukraine's ICBMs, if fired to hit a nearby (Russian) target, would probably burn up during their descent as the trajectory on which they would have to be fired would be so steep: the author is grateful to Dr Steven Miller of Harvard University for this point.

52 See Kuzio, *Ukraine, op. cit.* (n. 2 above), p. 33.

53 The author acknowledges Neil Malcolm's insight on this point. A significant rationalist element in the Russian political spectrum asserts that Russian territory should comprise those areas inhabited by Russians, which would include much of Kazakhstan.

54 *Inter alia*, the Ukrainian parliament insisted that all nuclear force assets on Ukrainian territory should be treated as Ukrainian, that Article V of the Lisbon Protocol was not to be binding on Ukraine, that Ukraine was to have administrative control over nuclear weapons on its territory, that it would move to non-nuclear weapon status once it had received security assurances from nuclear weapon states and guarantees of its borders, and that it should be compensated for missile dismantling costs and for any warhead components not returned to Ukraine. A full list of the conditions was published in *Trust and Verify: The Bulletin of the Verification Technology Information Centre*, no. 43, December 1993, p. 1.

55 Japan later announced that it would provide $117 million in aid for the nuclear disarmament involved. Russia would get 70% of the money, Ukraine 15%, Kazakhstan 10% and Belarus 5%; see 'Four Ex-Soviet States Share Japanese Aid', *Defense News*, 11–17 April 1994.

56 For the text of the agreement and some comment on it, see *Newsbrief* of the Programme for Promoting Nuclear Non-Proliferation at the University of Southampton, no. 25, 1st quarter 1994.

57 'Ukrainian warheads go', *Guardian*, 7 March 1994.

58 BBC *SWB* SU/1912 S1/1, 3 February 1994.

59 BBC *SWB* SU/1973 D/3, 16 April 1994.

60 The Kazakh ambassador in Iran was quoted in January 1994 as saying that 'Kazakhstan bears responsibility for its nuclear weapons itself. It does not intend to eliminate them or transfer them to other places until the non-use of such weapons is guaranteed at the world level and the planet gets rid of them'. However, the Russian government was reluctant to accept this report as accurate, see BBC *SWB* SU/1909 B/1, 31 January 1994.

61 BBC *SWB* SU/1935 S2/2, 2 March 1994.

62 The Harvard study cited above (n. 23) specified 8,800 tactical nuclear weapons. The Stockholm International Peace Research Institute (SIPRI) identified 14,405 Soviet nuclear systems (including anti-air missiles and sea-based systems) which were not covered by START (see 'Russia likely to become new nuclear superpower', *The Financial Times*, 28 August 1991). For other estimates see 'Nato will Soldaten bei der Sowjetunion-Hilfe einsetzen', *Frankfurter Allgemeine*, 20 December 1991.

63 Blair, *op. cit.*, p. 260, notes this as a possible vulnerable area for Russian controls.

64 Carnegie Endowment for International Peace/Monterey Institute of International Studies, *Nuclear Successor States of the Soviet Union*, Nuclear Weapons and Sensitive Export Status Report, no. 1, May 1994, pp. 12–13.

65 'Russia to Stop Producing Weapons-Grade Plutonium', *International Herald Tribune*, 18 March 1994.

66 Moscow Radio report in BBC *SWB* SU/1916 S2/1, 8 February 1994.

67 BBC *SWB* SU/1943 S1/2 11 March 1994.

68 The US anticipates that it will cost $8–9 billion to destroy its chemical weapons stock over a 10 to 15-year period. In 1993 Moscow felt that the cost of its equivalent operation would be about 500 billion roubles at August 1993 prices, with foreign countries hopefully contributing about 40% of the cost; see *Chemical Weapons Bulletin* no. 22, December 1993, 'News Chronology', 22 October 1993 and 26 November 1993. However Russia's estimate of the cost had seemingly gone up to 2,000 billion roubles by March 1994; see evidence of the Defence Ministry to the Russian Parliament, BBC *SWB* SU/1959 S1/1-2, 30 March 1994.

69 See *Chemical Weapons Bulletin*, no. 22, December 1993, 'News Chronology', 10 September 1993, 28–30 September 1993; *Chemical Weapons Bulletin*, no. 19, March 1993, 19 January 1993.

70 A.W. Krohn, 'The Challenge of Dumped Chemical Ammunition in the Baltic Sea', *Security Dialogue*, vol. 25, no. 1, March 1994, pp. 93–104, and a rejoinder by P.O. Granbum, pp. 105–10.

71 BBC *SWB* SU/1959 S1/2, 30 March 1994.

72 *Chemical Weapons Bulletin*, no. 19, March 1993, 'News Chronology', 17 November and 18–21 November 1992, *Chemical Weapons Bulletin*, no. 18, December 1992, 'News Chronology', 10–11 September 1992.

73 The estimates of Stephen Van Evera, 'Preventing War in the Former Soviet Empire', *Security Studies*, vol. 1, no. 3, spring 1992, p. 362.

74 For unsubstantiated reports of Iran's efforts to acquire FSU nuclear technology and technical experts, see 'Insider's Report', in *European Security Analyst*, October 1992.

75 See Blair, *op. cit.*, p. 15.

76 'Russia blocks scientists' departure', *Independent*, 10 February 1993.

77 'Most defence workers want to flee Russia', *Independent*, 12 October 1992.

78 Steven Miller, 'Western Diplomacy and the Soviet Nuclear Legacy', *Survival*, vol. 34, no. 3, autumn 1992, p. 5.

Chapter 3: Potential threats from military sector resources

1 Sergei Rogov, Deputy Director of the Institute of USA and Canada Studies in Moscow, presented this framework informally at the Wilton Park–Science Applications International joint conference on 'Planning for Security in the Changing International Environment' at Whiston House, Sussex, 20–24 April

1992. A further problem which he identified, settling the ownership of nuclear weapons, was discussed in Chapter 2.

2 See H. Gelman, *The Rise and Fall of National Security Decision-making in the Former USSR*, Santa Monica, CA, Rand, 1992.

3 Translation of the Russian Federation Law on Defence from *Krasnaya zvezda*, 10 October 1992, supplied by Sandhurst, SSRC, RMA, Advab. 832, November 1992. The Law made no mention of the role of the Russian Security Council.

4 'The West's fault or was it his?', *Independent on Sunday*, 14 March 1993.

5 See R.A. Wolf, *Russian High Command Appointments*, Sandhurst, RMA, June 1992; Pavel Baev, 'A Farewell to Arms Control? A View from Russia', *Bulletin of Arms Control*, no. 7, August 1992, p. 12. 'Starting from Zero?', in *International Defence Review*, vol. 25, no. 9, 1992, records Defence Minister Grachev's views on a civilian defence minister: he would not be competent to do the job and the military would not be able to understand such a choice – 'what is needed is a man who has a lifelong experience with the military' (p. 833). The article also lists seven deputy defence ministers; all save one (Professor Andrei Kokoshin) are professional soldiers (p. 834).

6 See 'New Yeltsin choice stresses continuity', *International Herald Tribune*, 16 December 1992.

7 'MPs curb Yeltsin's reforms', *Guardian*, 15 December 1992.

8 M.A. Smith, *The Russian Elections and Constitution: an Assessment*, Sandhurst, Conflict Studies Research Centre (CSRC), RMA, January 1994.

9 'Who runs Russia?', *The Economist*, 25 June 1994, pp. 35–6.

10 The Officers' Union leader, Stanislaw Terekhov, has said that his own organization has 3,000 members and enjoys the backing of 70–80% of the officer corps, see *RFE/RL Daily Report*, no. 51, 16 March 1993, p. 2.

11 Christopher Donnelly provides a vivid picture of the disorganization in the former Soviet armed forces, in 'Evolutionary Problems in the Former Soviet Armed Forces', *Survival*, vol. 34, no. 3, autumn 1992, but see 'Hidden enemy', *The Economist*, 27 March 1993, for a view that the military could yet intervene. According to some calculations, 3,000 of the best officers left the armed forces in 1992, there are about five murders and suicides a day in the armed forces, and about 120 conscripts a week may desert; see *RFE/RL Daily Report*, no. 51, 16 March 1993, p. 2.

12 'Besieged Yeltsin warns of "final option"', *Independent*, 3 March 1993.

13 B.D. Taylor, 'Russian Civil–Military Relations after the October Uprising', *Survival*, vol. 36, no. 1, spring 1994, pp. 3 and 20.

14 For the alleged independent actions of the commander of the 14th Army, Col. Gen. Aleksandr Lebed, see Wilbur E. Gray, *The Chivalrous Republic: Intrarepublic Conflict and the Case Study of Moldova*, Carlisle, PA, US Army War College, January 1993, pp. 14ff.

15 Coup rumours abounded in Moscow when President Yeltsin was first forced to

abandon Mr Gaidar as Prime Minister. 'Yeltsin stuns MPs by dropping Gaidar', *Independent*, 15 December 1992.

16 For a report on senior military leaders, including the 'Afghani' group in the defence ministry who favour a slowing down of economic reform, and on their support for the Civic Union and Vice-President Rutskoi, see 'Military men push Yeltsin towards conservative pact', *The Times*, 13 November 1992.

17 James Sherr, *op. cit.* (Chapter 2, n. 7 above), p. 1.

18 Philip Hanson, 'Russia: economic reform and local politics', *The World Today*, vol. 49, no. 4, April 1993, p. 64.

19 The Estonian Andrus Park has written that 'The possible dictatorship in Russia may be based on the principles of nationalism, xenophobia, fight against "Western imperialism" and transnational corporations, specific "Russian way" of development, non-marxist socialism, orthodox Church, market economy with strong state sector, welfare state, revival of Russian empire after the years of Gorbachevist defeatism and humiliation, even restoration of the monarchy, but the return to something based on the Communist ideology in its Leninist guise seems extremely unlikely': 'The Post-Soviet System of States', *Bulletin of Peace Proposals*, vol. 23, no. 1, 14 March 1992.

20 Sherr, *op. cit.*, p. 7.

21 See R.A. Wolf, *Ministry of Defence – Ukrainian Republic*, Sandhurst, RMA, July 1992.

22 Vigor and Orr, reporting Col.-Gen. Rodionov, *op. cit.* (Chapter 2, n. 5 above), p. 6.

23 See comments by Chief of the General Staff Kolesnikov, BBC *SWB* SU/1924 S1/2, 17 February 1994.

24 Domenick Bertelli, 'Defense Conversion in Russia', paper presented at the US International Studies Association Conference in Washington DC, March 1994, based on research in the Conversion Information Center, Council on Economic Priorities, New York, pp. 5–6.

25 The Russian Defence Ministry has said that 1.3 million conscripts cost 8 billion roubles in 1993 while the cost of 120,000 contract soldiers was 15 billion roubles; see BBC *SWB* SU/1924 S1/2, 17 February 1994. See also 'Funding Shortfalls Begin to Undermine Russian Military', *Defense News*, 21–27 February 1994.

26 Ruban, *op. cit.* (Chapter 2, n. 47 above).

27 BBC *SWB* SU/2030 S1/3, 24 June 1994.

28 T.R. Waters, *Military Reform or Military Disintegration in the Commonwealth – Russia: Hopes and Fears*, Sandhurst, RMA, April 1992, pp. 2 and 14.

29 Ruban, *op. cit.*

30 'Kravchuk stands firm on troops', *Independent*, 5 February 1992.

31 'Generals quit in row over appointment', *The Financial Times*, 24 February 1994.

32 Russian Defence Minister Grachev, asserting that coastal buildings and facilities were part of the Black Sea Fleet and thus not automatically Ukrainian property although on Ukrainian territory, said in April 1994 that 'Sevastopol should be the main base of the Russian Black Sea fleet. We believe that, besides Sevastopol,

Balaklava, Feodosiya, Kerch and Donuzlav should become the places for basing the fleet.' BBC *SWB* SU/1983 S1/2, 23 April 1994.

33 BBC *SWB* SU/1912 S1/4, 3 February 1994.

34 BBC *SWB* SU/2030 S1/4, 24 June 1994.

35 Waters, *op. cit.*, p. 5.

36 'Spoils of peace', *The Economist*, 21 March 1992.

37 'Sharing out the remnants of Soviet aviation' and 'Flying in the face of adversity', *Jane's Defence Weekly*, 17 April 1993.

38 In 1992 Russia claimed to have withdrawn from other countries some 80,000 servicemen and nearly 600,000 tons of materials and equipment; see Major General G. Ivanov, 'Reform in the Armed Forces: Results of the First Phase', *Military News Bulletin*, no. 12, December 1992.

39 See 'Fury as Red Army digs in', *The European*, 23–26 April 1992; and D.L. Clarke, 'Former Soviet Armed Forces in the Baltic States', *RFE/RL Research Report*, vol. 1, no. 16, 17 April 1992.

40 An Associated Press report used in 'CIS reaches two-speed agreement', *Independent*, 23 January 1993.

41 'Baltic pull-out row grows', *The Financial Times*, 1 April 1993.

42 See the Resolution printed in *Military News Bulletin* (from Novosti and the Russian Ministry of Defence), no. 12, December 1992.

43 Dmitri Steinberg, 'The Soviet Defence Burden: Estimating Hidden Defence Costs', *Soviet Studies*, vol. 44, no. 2, 1992, p. 259.

44 Former Russian Prime Minister Gaidar has said 62%; see 'Gaidar glimpses silver in the Russian cloud', *Independent*, 7 February 1993.

45 Bertelli, *op. cit.*, p. 3.

46 *Pravda* in BBC *SWB* SUW/0322 WD/7 4 March 1994; 'Russian Budget Ignites Protest', *Defense News*, 14–20 March 1994.

47 Taylor, *op. cit.* (n. 12 above), p. 16.

48 'Russian Budget Ignites Protest', *Defense News*, 14–20 March 1994.

49 'Military cuts put Yeltsin under threat', *Guardian*, 15 June 1994.

50 Major General Ivanov, in *Military News Bulletin*, December 1992, no. 12.

51 Interview with Col.-Gen. Vitaly Bologov, in *ibid.*

52 'A Nuclear Ukraine', RUSI *Newsbrief*, vol. 13, no. 2, February 1993, p. 13.

53 Quotation from the summary of the Ukrainian doctrine by C. J. Dick, *The Military Doctrine of Ukraine*, Sandhurst, CSRC, RMA, December 1993, p. 3.

54 *Ibid.*, pp. 6–12.

55 BBC *SWB* SU/1961 S1/5, 1 April 1994.

56 Julian Cooper, *The Conversion of the Former Soviet Defence Industry*, London, RIIA, Post-Soviet Business Forum, 1993, Chapter 5; Bertelli, *op. cit.*, notes some conversion successes in the FSU, as does K.M. Zisk, 'The Foreign Policy Preferences of Russian Defense Industrialists: Integration or Isolation', paper to US International Studies Association, Washington DC, March 1994, p. 16.

57 BBC *SWB* SUW/0330 WD/9, 29 April 1994.

58 Bertelli, *op. cit.*, p. 14 lists the following barriers to conversion in the FSU:

training and education limitations on market business norms, legal ambiguities regarding intellectual and physical property rights, the slow progress of privatization, lack of management expertise, financing problems, antiquated facilities, shortage of new product ideas, technology gaps, labour market inefficiencies, lack of marketing expertise, lack of quality control standards, broken supply networks, distribution problems, the influence of organized crime, bureaucratic red tape, and workers' attitudes.

59 Sherr, *op. cit.*, p. 3, stresses that without subsidies the defence sector would inevitably collapse at an unacceptable social cost.

60 Cooper, *op. cit.*, p. 5. See also P. Almquist, 'Arms Producers Struggle to Survive as Defense Orders Shrink', *RFE/RL Research Report*, vol. 2, no. 25, 18 June 1993, pp. 33–41.

61 Bertelli, *op. cit.*, p. 19.

62 Russia: New Stance on Conversion, *International Defense Review*, 3/93, p. 189; BBC *SWB* SUW/0322 WD/9, 4 March 1994.

63 Sonia Ben Ouagrham, *Le Désarmement et la conversion de l'industrie militaire en Russie*, UNIDIR Research Paper no. 24, Geneva, UNIDIR, 1993, p. 79.

64 Viktor Glukhikh, Chairman of the Russian State Committee for the Defence Industry, BBC *SWB* SU/0327 WD/10, 8 April 1994.

65 BBC *SWB* SUW/0318 WD/13, 4 February 1994. For a lengthy report sympathetic to the defence industries' predicament, see a *Pravda* account in BBC *SWB* SUW/0322 WD/7, 4 March 1994.

66 *Nuclear Successor States of the Soviet Union*, *op. cit.* (Chapter 2, no. 64 above), pp. 29–40; BBC *SWB* SU/2030 B/1, 24 June 1994; BBC *SWB* SU/2021 B/2, 14 June 1994.

67 Mikhail V. Berdennikov, 'Russia and her Security Policies', *The RUSI Journal*, vol. 137, no. 6, December 1992, p. 5.

68 Gray, *op. cit.* (n. 14), pp. 14–15; 'The Jane's Interview', *Jane's Defence Weekly*, 6 February 1993.

69 Berdennikov, *op. cit.*, p. 9.

70 BBC *SWB* SU/1927 C/3, 21 February 1994.

71 'The Jane's Interview', *op. cit.*

72 BBC *SWB* SUW/0322 WD8 4 March 1994; 'Expanding exports', *Jane's Defence Weekly*, 12 March 1994; BBC *SWB* SU/1907 S1/1, 28 January 1994; BBC *SWB* SU 03271 WD/10, 8 April 1994. For details of Rosvooruzhenie's mainly military leading personnel, see BBC *SWB* SUW/0325 WD/8, 25 March 1994.

73 BBC *SWB* SU/1929 S1/2, 23 February 1994.

74 BBC *SWB* SUW/0337 WD/4, 17 June 1994.

75 '180 submarines to go', *Jane's Defence Weekly*, 5 June 1993. There are two particularly problematic old submarine reactors stuck in the Russian naval base in Paldiski, Estonia, which the Russians should evacuate by 31 August 1994. Foreign aid may be made available for their dismantlement and removal. See BBC *SWB* SU/1989 E/1, 5 May 1994.

76 'Military cuts put Yeltsin under threat', *Guardian*, 15 June 1994.

77 Donnelly, *op. cit.* (n. 11 above), p. 30.

78 See CIS official data published in 'Fear of sharing a bed with the Russian elephant', *The Financial Times*, 20 January 1993.

79 BBC *SWB* SUW/0320 WA/2, 18 February 1994; see also 'Russia in deep crisis as output plunges by 25%', *The Financial Times*, 6 May 1994.

80 'Russia reborn: a survey of Russia', *The Economist*, 5 December 1992, p. 4. For further optimism, see 'Hartman Heartened By Visit to Russia', *Update of the Center for Foreign Policy Development*, Brown University, vol. 7, no. 2, January 1993, p. 4; and 'Never say die', *The Economist*, 27 March 1993.

81 For pessimism, see NATO Economic Committee, *Soviet Economic Performance in 1991: A Weak Foundation for a New Political Beginning*, Brussels, NATO, February 1992.

Chapter 4: Political problems and military solutions?

1 Listed in C.J. Dick, J.F. Dunn and J.B.K. Lough, *Potential Sources of Conflict in Post Communist Europe*, Occasional Brief no. 15, Sandhurst, SSRC, RMA, December 1992.

2 SIPRI has identified 30 territorial disputes in the Caucasus alone; see 'The empire splits up', *The Financial Times*, 22 December 1992.

3 See J.C. Oliphant, *Nationalities Problems in the Former Soviet Union*, Sandhurst, RMA, June 1992, for a similar breakdown of minority problems.

4 Stephen Van Evera, 'Preventing War in the Former Soviet Empire', *Security Studies*, vol. 1, no. 3, spring 1992, p. 364.

5 Hélène Carrère d'Encausse, *The End of the Soviet Empire: The Triumph of the Nations*, New York, Basic Books, 1993.

6 The goal of the National Radical Party, a breakaway from the LDP, is 'to unite Russians in one state': 'Eddie's right-wing chapter shocks Russian readers', *Independent on Sunday*, 24 January 1993.

7 For a discussion of these and other issues related to the political–economic future of Russia, see Neil Malcolm, 'Reconstructing Russia', *The World Today*, vol. 48, no. 10, October 1992, pp. 183–7.

8 The responsible Russian minister, Sergei Shakhray, has said that 365,000 ethnic Russians had migrated back to Russia from Central Asia in recent years. He expressed fears of three million immigrants, including from Ukraine. BBC *SWB*, SU/1960 B15, 31 March 1994.

9 See Oliphant, *op. cit.*, for a forceful assertion of this point.

10 D. Stenseth, 'The New Russia, CIS and the Future', *Security Dialogue*, vol. 23, no. 3, September 1992, p. 21.

11 Alexander Likhotal (of the Gorbachev Foundation) has observed that 'Russia, strictly speaking, ceased to be a normal state in the 16th century, when it gradually turned into an international subsystem, shaping the relations of dozens of nations, bearing the form of a state', in 'The New Russia and Eurasia', *Security Dialogue*, vol. 23, no. 3, September 1992, pp. 10–11.

12 Malcolm, *op. cit.*, p. 184; Oliphant, *op. cit.*, p. 6.

13 *The Financial Times* headline, 'Yakuts ponder identity in post-Soviet world' (27–28 March 1993) in some ways captured the essence of post-Cold War Russia, reflecting as it did the aspirations for independence of a group that few in the West had heard of.

14 Stenseth, *op. cit.*, p. 24. See also Steve Crawshaw, *Goodbye to the USSR: The Collapse of Soviet Power*, London, Bloomsbury, 1993, pp. 238–9.

15 D.P. Moynihan, *Pandaemonium: Ethnicity in International Relations*, Oxford, Oxford University Press, 1993. Without specifically discussing Russia, he forecasts that between 50 and 150 new states will come into being in the next 50 years (p. 168).

16 The Russian journalist Alexei Pankin argued this line at a talk at Chatham House on 7 May 1992. *The Economist*, in its 'Russia reborn: a survey of Russia', 5 December 1992, argued that economic interdependence limited the chances of the disintegration of Russia, but an important source of autonomy demands is the wish of local areas to hold on to most of their revenues from their raw material production.

17 'Meek revolt transforms Sverdlesh', *Independent*, 14 July 1993.

18 See for instance, BBC *Summary of World Broadcasts*: 7 July 1993, SU/1734 B/5; 14 July 1993, SU/1740 B/13; 20 July 1993, SU/1745 B4; 26 July 1993, SU/1750 B6; 21 July 1993, SU/1746 B/4; FBIS-SOV 93-128; 7 July 1993, pp. 38–9, FBIS-SOV-93-129; 8 July 1993, p. 36, FBIS-SOV-93-130; FBIS-SOV-93-132 13 July 1993, p. 55.

19 The text is published in BBC *SWB* SU/1985 S2/1, 30 April 1994, with various comments being published in the next issues of the *SWB*.

20 J.E. Stern, 'Moscow Meltdown: Can Russia Survive?', *International Security*, Spring 1994, vol. 18, no. 4, p. 40.

21 See John Morrison, 'Pereyaslev and After: The Russian–Ukrainian Relationship', *International Affairs*, vol. 69, no. 4, October 1993, pp. 677–704.

22 'Black Sea dispute over', *Jane's Defence Weekly*, 26 June 1993; 'Russia lays claim to Sevastopol', *Guardian*, 10 July 1993; 'Rich nations snub Yeltsin attempt to join the club', *Independent*, 10 July 1993; 'Russia's Foreign Policy Concept's Spheres of Interest', *Newsbrief*, RUSI, vol. 13, no. 7, July 1993, p. 52.

23 See for example 'Ukraine baulks at the painful cost of freedom', *Independent on Sunday*, 30 January 1994.

24 Peter van Ham, *Ukraine, Russia and European Security: Implications for Western Policy*, Chaillot Paper no. 13, Paris, WEU Institute for Security Studies, February 1994.

25 'Russian-Ukraine tensions ease', *The Financial Times*, 8 June 1994.

26 BBC *SWB* SU/1962 H/1, 4 April 1994; BBC *SWB* SU/1959 B/6, 30 March 1994.

27 'Belarus looks to Moscow', *Newsbrief*, RUSI, May 1993, vol. 13, no. 5, p. 36.

28 Vitaly Churkin, Russian Deputy Foreign Minister, BBC *SWB* SU/1940 B/3, 8 March 1994.

29 However, the *Independent* suggested a figure of 50,000: 'CIS reaches two-speed agreement', *Independent*, 23 January 1993. An Estonian official told the author in early 1993 that there were perhaps 9,000 Russian troops left in his country. A UK publication, without citing references, said in the summer of 1993 that there were only 7,600 Russian troops in Estonia, 2,200 in Latvia, and up to 10,000 in Lithuania; see C. Birch (ed.), *Russia: A State of Emergency*, London, Centre for Defence Studies, 1993, p. 26. In July 1994 the *Independent* estimated 10,500 in Latvia and 2,500 in Estonia: 'Clinton backs Baltics with strong freedom signals', *Independent*, 7 July 1994.

30 BBC *SWB* SU/1986 S2/5, 2 May 1994.

31 BBC *SWB* SU/1978 E/1, 22 April 1994.

32 See Prime Minister Chernomyrdin quoted in 'Russia confirms Baltic pull-out', *Jane's Defence Weekly*, 19 March 1994.

33 For Estonian thinking, see BBC *SWB*/1988 8/1, 4 May 1994.

34 For a striking account of groups and potential conflicts, see C.W. Blandy, 'A Compendium of Conflict in the Caucasus', Brief no. 1 and Brief no. 2, Sandhurst, SSRC, RMA, March 1993. As a sample of a much wider problem, it is notable that Dagestan comprises Avars, Russians, Dagyns, Kumyks, Lezghins, Laks, Azerbaijanis, Tabarasins, Chechens, Nogai, Rutuls, Aguls and Tats (Blandy, p. 12).

35 For details of this dispute see the Memorandum from the Institute of Social and Political Science, Charles University, Prague, on 'Military developments in Central and Eastern Europe and their political and diplomatic implications', May 1992.

36 See E. Foster, 'Mediators for Transcaucasia's Conflicts', *The World Today*, vol. 49, no. 5, pp. 89–92.

37 For doubts about the Moldavians' wish for unity with Romania, see the Memorandum from Charles University, *op. cit.*

38 BBC *SWB* SU/1971 D/4, 14 April 1994.

39 BBC *SWB* SU/1976 D/8, 20 April 1994.

40 Wilbur E. Gray, *The Chivalrous Republic: Intrarepublic conflict and the case study of Moldova*, Carlisle, PA, US Army War College, January 1993, pp. 9–10.

41 Cited in 'Myriad territorial disputes set to take centre stage', a piece which noted 14 such disputes, see *The Financial Times* 28 August 1991; see also C.J. Dick, J.F. Dunn and J.B.K. Lough, 'Pandora's Box: Potential Sources of Conflict in Post-communist Europe', *International Defense Review*, March 1993, pp. 203–8.

42 Gray, *op. cit.*, p. 1.

43 Carrère d'Encausse, *op. cit.* (n. 5), p. 102. See also K. Rupesinghe, P. King and O. Vorkunoja, *Ethnicity and Conflict in a Post-Communist World*, London, St Martin's Press, 1992.

44 President Nabiyev held office when Tajikistan first became independent. He was overthrown by Islamist forces which in turn were driven from power by Russian-backed units.

45 See Roland Dannreuther, *Creating New States in Central Asia*, Adelphi Paper 288, London, IISS/Brassey's, 1994, especially pp. 25–31.

46 M. Shashenkov, 'Security Issues in the Ex-Soviet Central Asian Republics', *London Defence Studies*, no. 14, London, Brasseys, 1992, p. 68.

47 Private source in the Russian government.

48 P. Kennedy, *Preparing for the Twenty-First Century*, New York, Vintage Books, 1993, pp. 242–9. See also P. Ferdinand (ed.), *The New Central Asia and its Neighbours*, London, RIIA/Pinter, 1994.

49 See B.V. Souders and R.E. Kanet, *An Emerging Inter-State System: Russia and the Other Former Republics of the USSR*, Occasional Paper, Urbana, IL, University of Illinois, September 1992. A former US diplomat, Harold Saunders, has further argued that the nature of these international relationships will be shaped by a range of factors, including historical experience, the formation of core concerns, the interaction of perceptions and the activities of non-governmental groups as well as governments. Harold H. Saunders, *The Concept of Relationship: A Perspective on the Future between the United States and the Successor States to the Soviet Union*, Columbus, OH, The Mershon Centre, Ohio State University, January 1993, pp. 18–19.

50 See, for instance, 'Back to the USSR', *Independent on Sunday*, 23 January 1994; 'Russia reaches out', *The Economist*, 26 February 1994; 'Kozyrev raises spectre of resurgent Russia', *Independent*, 24 February 1994. For an analysis that a consensus is emerging on Russia's primary concern with the near abroad, see Neil Malcolm, 'The New Russian Foreign Policy', *The World Today*, vol. 50, no. 2, February 1994, pp. 28–32. For a clear analysis of foreign policy debates in Russia, see A.G. Arbatov, 'Russia's Foreign Policy Alternatives', *International Security*, fall 1993, vol. 18, no. 2, pp. 5–43.

51 Z. Brzezinski, *Out of Control*, New York, Collier, pp. 167–81.

52 He argues that formerly families in great-power states were larger, with five to six children, and fatal disease was a common feature of young life: 'When it was normal to lose one or more children to disease, the loss of one or more youngsters in war had a different meaning'. He quotes the Italian term 'mammismo' ('motherism') to explain why 'no advanced low-birth rate countries can play the role of a classic great power role any more'. See 'Where Are the Great Powers?', *Foreign Affairs*, vol. 73, no. 4, July/August 1994, pp. 23–9.

53 In particular see views of Deputy Foreign Minister Aleksandr Panov on Chinese immigration into Russia, border problems, border troop levels and economic cooperation, BBC *SWB* SU/1982 B/6, 27 April 1994.

54 See Karen Dawisha and Bruce Parrott, *Russia and the New States of Eurasia*, Cambridge, Cambridge University Press, 1994, for a detailed examination of the main issues linking Russia and the other successor states of the former Soviet Union and of the main factors, including political developments in Russia, which will influence their handling.

55 Stenseth, *op. cit.* (n. 10 above), p. 24.

56 For an assessment of the limited prospects for the CIS, and a judgment that 'what can finally break-up the CIS is the ever growing tension between Russia and Ukraine', see Alexei Pushkow (Deputy Editor of *Moscow News*), 'The

Commonwealth of Independent States: Still alive though not kicking', *NATO Review*, no. 3 June 1992, pp. 13–18.

57 Text in *Military News Bulletin* from Novosti and the Russian Defence Ministry, no. 12, December 1992.

58 'CIS Move Stalls Pact On Security', *Defense News*, 21–27 June 1993.

59 BBC *SWB* SU/1940 S1/1, 8 March 1994.

60 See 'CIS summit ends in partial accord', *Guardian*, 23 January 1993, 'CIS reaches two-speed agreement' *Independent*, 23 January 1993.

61 Viktor Fedorchuk, 'From Dagomys to Yalta', *The Ukrainian Review*, autumn 1992, p. 5.

62 'Europe Relies on Stable CIS', *Defense News*, 9–15 November 1992.

63 CIS defence ministers agreed in March 1994 that Kazakhstan would send a battalion to Tajikistan 'in the near future' and that Kyrgyzstan would bring its unit there up to strength. Belarus refused to sign a statement on stabilizing the Tajik–Afghan border; see BBC *SWB* SU/1937 S1/6, 4 March 1994.

64 Likhotal, *op. cit.*, p. 11.

65 Roland Dannreuther, *op. cit.*, pp. 57 and 5. Arbatov, *op. cit*, p. 35, agrees that four Central Asian states will eventually move away from the CIS but stresses that Kazakhstan will remain 'an area of vital Russian interests for ethnic, economic and security reasons'. See also 'Central Asians cut loose from Moscow', *The Financial Times*, 27 January 1994, and 'Foreign investment pours into Kazakhstan', *The Financial Times*, 15 February 1994; 'Central Asian Republics look west for investment', *The Financial Times*, 1 February 1994.

66 'Russia finds independent foreign policy', *The Financial Times*, 21 March 1994.

Chapter 5: Western interests, approaches and priorities

1 See Trevor Taylor, *NATO and Central Europe: Problems and Opportunities in a New Relationship*, RIIA Discussion Paper No. 39, London, RIIA, 1992.

2 Russia did veto a resolution in May 1993 on transforming the funding of UNFICYP, the United Nations Force in Cyprus, so that it would be paid for according to a formula involving the UN membership as a whole, rather than the force-contributing states bearing the cost. However, it allowed the resolution to proceed soon after, once Greek Cyprus had agreed to pay a significant share of the UNFICYP cost.

3 'Moscow jolt: is Cold War back?', *International Herald Tribune*, 15 December 1992.

4 As anticipated in the Report of the North Atlantic Assembly Political Committee, Rapporteur Bruce George, on *NATO and the New Arc of Crisis* and *Dialectics of Russian Foreign Policy*, Brussels, NAA, November 1992, pp. 22–3.

5 Brzezinski, *op. cit.* (Chapter 4, n. 51 above), argues for the reverse priority. See p. 172.

6 For Henry Kissinger's and Zbigniew Brzezinski's association with the 'Russia last' approach because of its inherent instability, see T. Kuzio, *Ukraine: the*

Unfinished Revolution, London, Institute for European Defence and Strategic Studies (European Security Study No. 16), p. 36.

7 See 'Red-tape and suspicion slow nuclear dismantling to a crawl', *Independent*, 15 March 1993.

8 Bruce Blair, *The Logic of Accidental Nuclear War*, Washington DC, Brookings Books, April 1993, pp. 264–5.

9 'Non-Proliferation, International Security and US Interests', A Policy Statement by the Atlantic Council of the United States, December 1992. The statement also said that the US should 'work to reinforce negative security assurances by announcing a policy of no-first use of nuclear weapons'.

10 See T. Taylor, *op. cit.*, pp. 19–20.

11 Lynn E. Davis, *An Arms Control Strategy for the New Europe*, Santa Monica, Rand Corp., 1993, p. 26.

12 Brzezinski, *op. cit.*, p. x.

13 For the West to threaten to initiate nuclear war for the defence of Central Europe would lack credibility in the light of the history of the Cold War and would be less acceptable to Western European and North American publics than a commitment to defend that region against conventional forces with conventional forces.

14 In this author's view, John Mearsheimer, in his 'The Case for a Ukrainian Nuclear Deterrent' (*Foreign Affairs*, vol. 72, no. 3, summer 1993, pp. 50–66) underestimates the technical problems of establishing a Ukrainian deterrent and the political/military difficulties inherent in Ukraine's transition to an operational nuclear weapons state. He also believes that international stability would be enhanced if other major states including Germany had their own nuclear forces. Far more persuasive is Steven Miller, 'The Case Against a Ukrainian Nuclear Deterrent', *Foreign Affairs*, vol. 72, no. 3, summer 1993, pp. 67–80, who argues that nuclear weapons generally are only one factor among many influencing whether a conflictual situation turns violent and do not make their possessors feel secure. Specifically, he argues that Ukrainian security would be weakened by an attempt to become a nuclear weapons state since (1) in the transition period Russia would be tempted to intervene, (2) many potential targets of Ukrainian missiles (i.e. Russia, Western Europe and North America) would define Ukraine as a threat, (3) Ukraine would initially not possess a comprehensive system, (4) in the long term it would always be strategically inferior to Russia, (5) Russia's nuclear forces would deter Ukraine's in almost all circumstances, (6) the cost of building a nuclear force would damage Ukrainian conventional forces, (7) a Ukrainian deterrent would damage arms control regimes which could help Ukraine, and (8) a Ukrainian nuclear force would damage relations with the West.

15 BBC *SWB* SU/1939 D/1, 7 March 1994.

16 Blair, *op. cit.*, pp. 263–4.

17 'Kravchuk hopes for aid package', *The Financial Times*, 9 May 1994.

18 T. Kuzio, *op. cit.*, p. 27.

19 US Majority Leader Richard Gephardt, 'A New Partnership: US Relations with Russia and the NIS', London, USIS/US Embassy, 26 April 1993.

20 See speech of William Dircks, Deputy Director General of the IAEA, at Chatham House on 4 November 1992.

21 Dircks, *ibid.*, advocated this approach.

22 'US and Russia reach accord on inspecting plutonium sites', *International Herald Tribune*, 17 March 1994.

23 It can, with difficulty, be changed into a mixed oxide fuel form. Alternatively, it could be burned in specially designed (fast breeder) reactors, a solution yet to be developed but which Japan is keen to explore. Weapons-grade uranium (uranium 235 enriched to a concentration above 90%) can simply be mixed with natural uranium to yield a fuel suitable for use in most civil nuclear power generators. Finally it can be vitrified and stored, most obviously deep underground.

24 Von Hippel et al., 'Eliminating Nuclear Warheads', *Scientific American*, August 1993, pp. 32–7.

25 The IAEA calculates that the FSU will have enough spare fissionable material to meet all Western civil reactor needs for five years.

26 The West can scarcely complain about Russia's efforts to sell aircraft in the Gulf and to Malaysia; for instance, see 'Malaysia may buy $700m Mig fighters', *The Financial Times*, 3 March 1993; 'Russia's arms sale drive triumphs', *The Financial Times*, 6 June 1994.

27 'Russia agrees to sell arms to Syria', *Guardian*, 29 April 1994. For the problems of a proposed deal with Turkey, see 'Money problems ... "cost free" arms deal', *Jane's Defence Weekly*, 27 February 1993, p. 13 and 'Cost-free rescue bid', *Jane's Defence Weekly*, 6 March 1993, p. 11. India needs around 100,000 spare parts for its Soviet equipment, see 'Belarus To Fortify Indian Armor', *Defense News*, 31 May–6 June 1993.

28 Viktor Glukhikh, Chairman of the Russian State Committee for the Defence Industry, has said that Russian arms exports rose by 11.7% in 1993 to $2.15 billion. Russia dealt with only 26 customers, rather than the 52 which the Soviet Union once served, and he argued that it should concentrate its sales efforts on the CIS. This would obviously yield little hard currency. The Rosvorhuzheniye arms export company recognized that it would take a long time to build up Russian arms sales; see BBC *SWB* SU/1973 D/3, 16 April 1994 and SUW/0328 WD/7, 15 April 1994; BBC *SWB* SUW/0323 WD/10, 11 March 1994. The Russian Minister of Foreign Economic Relations, Oleg Davidov, said that Russian arms exports were worth only $1.2 billion in 1993. He may have been referring to deliveries rather than orders: see 'Russian exports to rise', *Jane's Defence Weekly*, 15 January 1994.

29 '"Soviet" arms exports fading', *Jane's Defence Weekly*, 26 June 1993.

30 'East/West Aerospace Ventures on the Rise', *Aviation Week and Space Technology*, 23 August 1993; noted by K.M. Zisk, 'The Foreign Policy Preferences of Russian Defense Industrialists', paper to US International Studies Association, Washington DC, 30 March 1993.

31 S.J. Blank, *Challenging the New World Order: The Arms Transfer Policies of the Russian Republic*, Carlisle, PA, US Army War College, October 1993. For Russian ambitions in the arms trade, see BBC *SWB* SUW/0311 WD11, 10 December 1993.

32 Quoted in C.J. Dick, 'Russia's Draft Military Doctrine, 10 Months On', *SSRC Occasional Brief*, no. 17, Sandhurst, RMA, April 1993, p. 2.

33 Stephen Van Evera, 'Preventing War in the Former Soviet Empire', *Security Studies*, vol. 1, no. 3, spring 1992, p. 370, acknowledges but rejects this option.

34 'Prospects in the pipeline', *The Financial Times*, 27 March 1994; 'Azerbaijan oil deal back on track', *The Financial Times*, 23 February 1994; 'Russians muscle in on oil deals', *The Financial Times*, 21 January 1994; 'Azerbaijan to sign oil deal with BP to ward off Russia', *Independent*, 12 February 1994; and 'Kazakhs refuse Russia oil and gas equity stakes', *The Financial Times*, 23 March 1994.

35 'Ukraine rebuffs Yeltsin', *Independent*, 2 March 1993.

36 See J.B.K. Lough, *The Russian Army Enters Politics*, Sandhurst, SSRC, RMA, July 1992, quoting *Sovetskaya Rossiya*, 7 July 1992. Also Georgian leader Eduard Shevardnadze has accused Russian forces of arming Abkhazian rebels in Georgia: *RFE/RL Daily Report*, no. 52, 17 March 1993, p. 2.

37 See interview with General Leonid Ivashov, Secretary General to the CIS Council of Ministers, *Defense News*, 1–7 March 1993.

38 D. Hurd and A. Kozyrev, 'Challenge of Peacekeeping', *The Financial Times*, 14 December 1993.

39 See, for instance, 'Russia insists on solo intervention', *Guardian*, 25 June 1994.

40 Dick, *op. cit.*, p. 2.

41 'Russia finds independent foreign policy', *The Financial Times*, 21 March 1994.

42 For a discussion of possibilities short of dual citizenship for 'Russians' living outside Russia, see Neil Melvin, *Forging the New Russian Nation: Russian Foreign Policy and the Russian-Speaking Communities of the Former USSR*, Discussion Paper no. 50, London, Royal Institute of International Affairs, 1994, especially pp. 49–54.

43 Richard Dalton, 'The role of the CSCE' in Hugh Miall (ed.), *Minority Rights in Europe: The Scope for a Transnational Regime*, London, RIIA/Pinter, 1994.

44 BBC *SWB* SU/1917 D/8, 9 February 1994.

45 BBC *SWB* SU/1920 E/6, 12 February 1994.

46 James F. Holcomb, quoting the Russian General Staff, *Russian Military Doctrine*, Sandhurst, RMA, August 1992, p. 3.

47 'Russia energy deals gather pace', *The Financial Times*, 24 June 1994. A sea of deals have been arranged but must await the Russian parliament approving an overall law to govern them before implementation can occur.

48 See Richard K. Betts, 'Systems for Peace or Causes of War? Collective Security, Arms Control and the New Europe', *International Security*, vol. 17, no. 1, summer 1992, pp. 5–43; see also critical comment on his arguments by Michael J. Mazaar, and Betts's replies in 'A Farewell to Arms Control', *International Security*, vol. 17, no. 3, winter 1992/3, pp. 188–200.

49 For a negative view of the prospects of existing agreements, see Pavel K. Baev,

'Farewell to Arms Control? A View from Russia', *Bulletin of Arms Control*, no. 7, August 1992, pp. 8–13.

50 Ivo Daalder has argued that 'cooperative arms control' among states with 'largely compatible political interests' can help 'to transform political relations in a matter conducive to creating a pluralistic security community', in 'Cooperative Arms Control: A New Agenda for the Post-Cold War Era', *CISSM Papers* 1, Center for International and Security Studies at Maryland, University of Maryland, October 1992, p. 9.

51 They were advocated in Davis, *op. cit.*

52 Russian Chief of the General Staff Mikhail Koleznikov, BBC *SWB* SU/1977 S1/1-3, 21 April 1994.

53 S.J. Blank, *Russia and the Baltic: Is there a threat to European Security?*, Carlisle, PA, US Army War College, March 1993, p. 16.

54 'Baltic states will take part in US exercise', *Jane's Defence Weekly*, 12 June 1993.

55 A presentation by Michael Brown, 'The End of Arms (Control)?', *Arms Control Brief*, vol. 1, no. 1. See also Blair, *op. cit.*, pp. 5, 268.

56 'Zero ballistic missiles in a Third World Context', *Arms Control Brief*, vol. 1, no. 2, December 1992.

57 Many tactical nuclear warheads have already been put into storage and strategic bombers have been taken off alert status. See also 'Reduce Doomsday readiness, say US defence experts', *Guardian*, 10 October 1993.

58 These paragraphs draw heavily on the thinking in Blair, *op. cit.*

59 *Military News Bulletin*, no. 12, December 1992 reports a CIS resolution at Bishek in October 1992.

60 M.V. Berdennikov, 'Russia and her Security Policies', *The RUSI Journal*, vol. 137, no. 6, December 1992, p. 8.

61 'US, Russia Initiate Talks on Scud Defense', *Defense News*, 22–28 February 1993.

62 Private sources and 'THAAD May Be Treaty Debate Fulcrum', *Defense News*, 11–17 April 1994.

63 BBC *SWB* SU/2023 F/1, 16 June 1994.

64 'Gaidar glimpses silver in Russian cloud', *Independent*, 7 February 1993.

65 Andrus Park, 'The Post-Soviet System of States', *Bulletin of Peace Proposals*, voi. 23, no. 1, 14 March 1992, p. 15.

66 See Stephen Van Evera, 'Preventing War in the Former Soviet Empire', *Security Studies*, vol. 1, no. 3, spring 1992, p. 368.

67 See C.J. Dick, J.F. Dunn and J.B.K. Lough, 'Pandora's Box: Potential Sources of Conflict in Post-communist Europe', *International Defense Review*, March 1993, p. 203.

68 This issue is discussed in Julian Cooper, *The Conversion of the Former Soviet Defence Industry*, London, RIIA, Post-Soviet Business Forum, 1993.

69 *Ibid.*

70 *Ibid.*, p. 35.

71 *The Russian Defense Business Directory* was published by the US Commerce Department in November, see 'US Gives Advice on Russia' *Defense News*, 30

November–6 December 1992.

72 'US OKs Funding for Joint Russian Radar Project', *Defense News*, 14–20 February 1994.

73 'West Europeans Push Conversion Plan for Russia', *Defense News*, 28 February–6 March 1994.

74 A. Kennaway puts the identification of exportable products, alongside the generation of a comprehensive business plan and the tutoring and reorganization of workforces, at the centre of his ideas for conversion; see his *Rehabilitation of a Russian Military Factory*, Sandhurst, CSRC, RMA, December 1993. He also advocates the demilitarization of the whole science and technology community in the FSU: see *Towards a Rational Philosophy for Science and Engineering in the Former Soviet Union*, Sandhurst, CSRC, RMA, 1994.

75 See Paul Humes Folta, *From Swords to Plowshares: Defense Industry Reform in the PRC*, Boulder, CO, Westview Press, 1992.

76 'Perry Sells Conversion Plan to Former Soviets', *Defense News*, 28 March–4 April 1994.

77 See Kennaway, *op. cit.*, for a more detailed approach to these issues.

78 The number of products on the Cocom Industrial List had been considerably reduced even by the summer of 1992.

79 M. Cernicek, T. Copeland and S. Garber, 'Building New Bridges: Technology Transfer and East–West Stability', *Ridgway Viewpoints*, no. 93–1, Pittsburgh, PA, University of Pittsburgh (undated).

80 There have been concerns that the US was seeking to link national economic gain to easing Cocom restrictions, as many Western European businessmen feel it always has. For a hint of US pressure, note Warren Christopher's words that 'Cold War laws and regulations ... were meant to restrict trade with a communist Soviet Union but now they only impede our relations with a democratic Russia. To the maximum extent possible, consistent with America's interests, US markets should be open to competitive Russian products. Similarly, Americans should be allowed to export our goods and technology to Russia.' 'US will shoulder responsibility for world leadership', speech in Minnesota published by USIS, London, 28 May 1993.

81 Jonathan Steele, 'Farewell Uncle Vanya', *Guardian Weekend*, 2 April 1994, p. 27.

82 Alexander Likhotal, 'The New Russia and Eurasia', *Security Dialogue*, vol. 23, no. 3, September 1992, p. 16.

83 'E Europe expects more from EBRD', *The Financial Times*, 2 March 1993.

84 'Excess gives way to restraint', *The Financial Times*, 4 March 1994.

85 In the summer of 1993, the US and Russia agreed that joint peacekeeping exercises should be held and designated the units involved: see 'Russia/US to train for peacekeeping', *Jane's Defence Weekly*, 19 June 1993. However, in the spring of 1994 President Yeltsin reportedly cancelled the ground forces exercises with the US amidst Russian nationalist claims about US spying on Russia: see 'Yeltsin ditches former allies', *Guardian*, 29 April 1994. See also BBC *SWB* SU/1959 S1/4, 30 March 1994; BBC *SWB* SU/1954 S1/2, 24 March 1994. In

March 1993 Russia, the US and Canada completed a search and rescue exercise in the Arctic; see 'Russians join US SAR exercise', *Jane's Defence Weekly*, 2 April 1994. For the details of the Russian–German military cooperation agreement, see 'Ruehe Steps Up German Presence', *Defense News*, 19–25 April 1993 and 'Germany hosts Grachev', *Jane's Defence Weekly*, 19 March 1994. Britain and Russia have also agreed on a joint ground forces exercise.

86 See General Pavel Grachev, 'The Defence Policy of the Russian Federation', *RUSI Journal*, vol. 137, no. 5, October 1992, p. 7. For details of the Russian–British Military Contacts programme between 1992 and 1994, including defence staff discussions, exchange visits of paratroop units, warships, military schools and military bands, see *Military News Bulletin* of Novosti and the Russian Defence Ministry, no. 12, December 1992.

87 'Russia Readies Partnership for Peace Details', *Defense News*, 4–10 April 1994. Russia also wants to send a political liaison team to NATO headquarters at Evere, Belgium, and a military liaison group to SHAPE at Mons. See also BBC *SWB* SU/1953 S/1-2, 23 March 1994.

88 'Finances Hold Key to NATO–East Joint Peace-keeping', *Defense News*, 22–28 March 1993.

89 See, for instance, 'Fight for the final frontier', *The Financial Times*, 2 February 1993.

90 'Eurocopter signs Russian deal', *The Financial Times*, 20 January 1993.

91 'Cocom Adds Export Control Aid Package For East Bloc', *Defense News*, 30 November–6 December 1992.

Chapter 6: The institutional dimensions of Western policy

1 S. Van Evera, 'Preventing War in the Former Soviet Empire', *Security Studies*, vol. 1, no. 3, p. 373.

2 By the summer of 1993, both Russia and the United States had moratoria in place. Russia's dated back to the collapse of the Soviet Union, which meant that it lost access to test facilities in Kazakhstan. President Clinton announced a US 15-month testing moratorium in June 1993 and extended it in March 1994.

3 'Kohl backs Ukraine in fight for EC markets', *The Financial Times*, 11 June 1993.

4 EC Copenhagen Summit, 21–22 June 1993, *Conclusions of the Presidency*, para. 10, noted that 'The European Council expressed keen interest in expanding cooperation with Ukraine. Substantial progress towards the fulfilment by Ukraine of its commitments under the Lisbon protocol to ratify START 1 and to accede to the NPT as a non-nuclear weapons state is essential for Ukraine's full integration into the international community and would promote the development of its relations with the Community and its Member States'.

5 There are a variety of functions which Cocom's successor could pursue but it will certainly have to bring in Russia and Ukraine; and whatever tasks it undertakes will benefit from the new participants having effective export control machinery. To provide guidance on this subject see Owen Greene, 'Successor to Cocom', Bristol, Saferworld Briefing, March 1994.

6 'Estonia bows to pressure', *Independent*, 8 July 1993; BBC *SWB* SU/1920 E/6, 12 February 1994.

7 See Klaus Schumann, 'The role of the Council of Europe', in Hugh Miall (ed.), *Minority Rights in Europe: The Scope for a Transnational Regime*, London, RIIA/Pinter, 1994; 'Britain obstructs action on Minority rights', *Independent*, 13 July 1993; Council of Europe Summit, *Vienna Declaration*, 9 October 1993.

8 Although there is some confusion as to whether subjects for a common European foreign and security policy were agreed at Maastricht, since nothing appeared in the final treaty documentation, the wording of the Lisbon communiqué made clear that the member states wanted to move towards a common policy on the former Soviet Union, on the CSCE, and on defence-related exports.

9 It accepted at its Oslo summit in June 1992 that it could provide peacekeeping forces under a CSCE mandate. It was agreed in November 1992 that it could also provide such forces for UN missions.

10 Report to Ministers by the NACC Ad Hoc Group on Peacekeeping for the NACC meeting in Athens, 11 June 1993, published by NATO Press Service, Brussels, 11 June 1993.

11 The CSCE endorsed this rule in July 1992.

12 Peter van Ham, *Ukraine, Russia and European Security: Implications for Western Policy*, Chaillot Paper no. 13, Paris, WEU Institute for Security Studies, February 1994, p. 57, notes that the CSCE Secretariat was asked at the December 1993 CSCE ministerial meeting to draft rules to govern peacekeeping in the FSU.

13 For a somewhat less gloomy view, see Julian Cooper, *The Conversion of the Former Soviet Defence Industry*, London, RIIA, Post-Soviet Business Forum, 1993.

14 See the 1993 Work Plan for Dialogue, Partnership and Cooperation, *NATO Review*, February 1993, p. 31.

15 See Cooper, *op. cit.*, p. 32.

16 The first Chiefs of Staff meeting was held in April 1992 and the second a year later.

17 K.M. Zisk, *Civil–Military Relations in the New Russia*, Columbus, OH, The Mershon Centre, University of Ohio, March 1993, pp. 15–16.

18 'Disarray Characterises NACC Forum Projects', *Defense News*, 19 March–4 April 1993.

19 Quoted in 'Christopher, Kozyrev pledge to handle problems as equals', Reuters report in *Japan Times*, 15 March 1994.

20 Text of NATO–Russian Protocol on the PFP Agreement, BBC *SWB* SU/2029 B/1, 23 June 1994.

21 See, for instance, Karl Deutsch, *Political Community and the North Atlantic Area*, Princeton, NJ, Princeton University Press, 1957; R. Tooze, 'Communications Theory', in T. Taylor (ed.), *Approaches and Theory in International Relations*, London, Longman, 1978, pp. 205–36; R.L. Merritt and B.M. Russett, *From National Development to Global Community*, London, George Allen & Unwin, 1981, pp. 7–9.

INDEX

163

neutral and non–aligned states (NNA), 4, 127
New Zealand, 4
Non-Proliferation Treaty (NPT), 17, 20, 22, 24, 79
Non-Proliferation Treaty conference 1995, 17, 121
North Atlantic Cooperation Council (NACC), 78–9, 111, 123, 127, 128, 130, 131, 132, 133–4, 135, 136
North Atlantic Council, 124
North Korea, 27–8, 104
Northern Territories, 65, 131, 132
Norway, 9
nuclear capability (Russia), 14–15, 70, 77
nuclear deterrence, and Russian Federation, 66
nuclear disarmament, 79, 101–2
nuclear forces, 3, 17–18
nuclear fuel, Russia and Ukraine, 2
nuclear materials, trade in, 45, 82
Nuclear Planning Group, 122
nuclear proliferation, prevention, 81–90
Nuclear Proliferation Treaty (NPT) review conference 1995, 83
nuclear war, feasibility, as seen by Russians, 11
nuclear weapons, 15, 23, 27–8, 82, 83–4, 101–3, 120–1
 disposal problems, 47
 'no first use' policy, 118
 Russia and Ukraine, 55

Oberonexport organization, 46
Officers' Union, 32
Open Skies Treaty 1992, 79, 101
Organization for Economic Cooperation and Development (OECD), 4
Ossetians, 51

Paris Charter 1990 (CSCE), 74, 79, 90, 94
Partnership for Peace (PFP) agreements, 79, 111, 112, 118–19, 127–8, 130, 132, 133, 136, 137
peacekeeping forces, 112–13, 127
People's Party of Free Russia, 32
Perry, US Defense Secretary, 85
plutonium, 25, 87–8
Poland, 8, 123
 economy, 110
 and FSU, 71
 and NATO, 56, 74, 76, 94, 119
 and Russia, 55, 119
 troop withdrawals, 8
Poles, 50, 63

political system, Russia, 30–1
professionalism, Russian forces, 40–1, 112
proliferation, arms
 control, 72, 73
 direct threat to West, 8–16
 indirect threat by proliferation, 16–28
 prevention, 81–90, 122–4
Pskov Oblast (Latvia), 60

radiation dangers, 15–16
Rakhmonov, President Imomali, 63
refugees, potential, 70, 76, 77
Riga (Latvia), 60
Rodionov, Colonel-General I., 9
Rogov, Sergei, on the military, 29
Romania, 111, 123
 and Moldova, 62, 71
Romanians in Moldova, 50, 62
Rosvooruzheniye state company, 46
Rühe, Volker, 95
Russia, 138–9
 aid to, 76–7, 110–11
 armed forces, 8, 10, 43
 arms sales, 88–9
 authoritarianism, 33
 and Baltic states, 9, 13, 58–61
 and Belarus, 57–8
 biological weapons, 26–7
 Bishkek agreement, 66
 Black Sea Fleet, 2, 35–6
 break-up, 52–4
 bureaucracy, 81
 CFE Treaty, 38, 41, 95
 chemical weapons, 26
 and CIS, 9, 11–12, 39, 69
 and Cocom, 123–4
 and CSCE, 91, 129
 democratization, 110
 disengagement possible, 69
 economy, 48–9, 76–7, 114
 as part of Europe, 128
 and European Union, 139–40
 possible expansion, imperialism, 64–5, 77
 role in FSU, 90
 possible hostility, 16, 75–6
 intervention policy, 12
 and Japan, 61, 65, 131, 132
 and Kazakhstan, 22, 57
 and Lithuania, 2, 38, 59, 60
 military bases, 13, 39
 military doctrine, 9, 11, 12–13
 and NATO, 126
 effect of wider NATO membership, 95